Scott Foresman

Science

The Diamond Edition

PEARSON
Scott Foresman

Editorial Offices: Glenview, Illinois • Parsippany, New Jersey • New York, New York
Sales Offices: Boston, Massachusetts • Duluth, Georgia • Glenview, Illinois
Coppell, Texas • Sacramento, California • Mesa, Arizona
www.pearsonsuccessnet.com

Series Authors

Dr. Timothy Cooney
Professor of Earth Science and Science Education
University of Northern Iowa (UNI)
Cedar Falls, Iowa

Dr. Jim Cummins
Professor
Department of Curriculum, Teaching, and Learning
University of Toronto
Toronto, Canada

Dr. James Flood
Distinguished Professor of Literacy and Language
School of Teacher Education
San Diego State University
San Diego, California

Barbara Kay Foots, M.Ed.
Science Education Consultant
Houston, Texas

Dr. M. Jenice Goldston
Associate Professor of Science Education
Department of Elementary Education Programs
University of Alabama
Tuscaloosa, Alabama

Dr. Shirley Gholston Key
Associate Professor of Science Education
Instruction and Curriculum Leadership Department
College of Education
University of Memphis
Memphis, Tennessee

Dr. Diane Lapp
Distinguished Professor of Reading and Language Arts in Teacher Education
San Diego State University
San Diego, California

Sheryl A. Mercier
Classroom Teacher
Dunlap Elementary School
Dunlap, California

Karen L. Ostlund, Ph.D.
UTeach Specialist
College of Natural Sciences
The University of Texas at Austin
Austin, Texas

Dr. Nancy Romance
Professor of Science Education & Principal Investigator
NSF/IERI Science IDEAS Project
Charles E. Schmidt College of Science
Florida Atlantic University
Boca Raton, Florida

Dr. William Tate
Chair and Professor of Education and Applied Statistics
Department of Education
Washington University
St. Louis, Missouri

Dr. Kathryn C. Thornton
Former NASA Astronaut Professor
School of Engineering and Applied Science
University of Virginia
Charlottesville, Virginia

Dr. Leon Ukens
Professor Emeritus
Department of Physics, Astronomy, and Geosciences
Towson University
Towson, Maryland

Steve Weinberg
Consultant
Connecticut Center for Advanced Technology
East Hartford, Connecticut

ISBN–13: 978-0-328-28958-5 (SVE), ISBN–10: 0-328-28958-2 (SVE);
ISBN–13: 978-0-328-30434-9 (A), ISBN–10: 0-328-30434-4 (A);
ISBN–13: 978-0-328-30435-6 (B), ISBN–10: 0-328-30435-2 (B);
ISBN–13: 978-0-328-30436-3 (C), ISBN–10: 0-328-30436-0 (C);
ISBN–13: 978-0-328-30437-0 (D), ISBN–10: 0-328-30437-9 (D).

Photographs
Every effort has been made to secure permission and provide appropriate credit for photographic material. The publisher deeply regrets any omission and pledges to correct errors called to its attention in subsequent editions. Unless otherwise acknowledged, all photographs are the property of Scott Foresman, a division of Pearson Education. Photo locators denoted as follows: Top (T), Center (C), Bottom (B), Left (L), Right (R), Background (Bkgd)

Consulting Author

Dr. Michael P. Klentschy
Superintendent
El Centro Elementary School District
El Centro, California

Science Content Consultants

Dr. Frederick W. Taylor
Senior Research Scientist
Institute for Geophysics
Jackson School of Geosciences
The University of Texas at Austin
Austin, Texas

Dr. Ruth E. Buskirk
Senior Lecturer
School of Biological Sciences
The University of Texas at Austin
Austin, Texas

Dr. Cliff Frohlich
Senior Research Scientist
Institute for Geophysics
Jackson School of Geosciences
The University of Texas at Austin
Austin, Texas

Brad Armosky
McDonald Observatory
The University of Texas at Austin
Austin, Texas

NASA Content Consultants

Adena Williams Loston, Ph.D.
Chief Education Officer
Office of the Chief Education Officer

Clifford W. Houston, Ph.D.
Deputy Chief Education Officer for Education Programs
Office of the Chief Education Officer

Frank C. Owens
Senior Policy Advisor
Office of the Chief Education Officer

Deborah Brown Biggs
Manager, Education Flight Projects Office
Space Operations Mission Directorate, Education Lead

Erika G. Vick
NASA Liaison to Pearson Scott Foresman
Education Flight Projects Office

William E. Anderson
Partnership Manager for Education
Aeronautics Research Mission Directorate

Anita Krishnamurthi
Program Planning Specialist
Space Science Education and Outreach Program

Bonnie J. McClain
Chief of Education
Exploration Systems Mission Directorate

Diane Schweizer
Program Scientist
Earth Science Education

Deborah Rivera
Strategic Alliances Manager
Office of Public Affairs
NASA Headquarters

Douglas D. Peterson
Public Affairs Officer, Astronaut Office
Office of Public Affairs
NASA Johnson Space Center

Nicole Cloutier
Public Affairs Officer, Astronaut Office
Office of Public Affairs
NASA Johnson Space Center

Dr. Jennifer J. Wiseman
Hubble Space Scientist Program Scientist
NASA Headquarters

Reviewers

Dr. Maria Aida Alanis
Administrator
Austin ISD
Austin Texas

Melissa Barba
Teacher
Wesley Mathews Elementary
Miami, Florida

Dr. Marcelline Barron
Supervisor/K-12 Math
and Science
Fairfield Public Schools
Fairfield, Connecticut

Jane Bates
Teacher
Hickory Flat Elementary
Canton, Georgia

Denise Bizjack
Teacher Dr. N. H. Jones
Elementary
Ocala, Florida

Latanya D. Bragg
Teacher
Davis Magnet School
Jackson, Mississippi

Richard Burton
Teacher
George Buck Elementary
School 94
Indianapolis, Indiana

Dawn Cabrera
Teacher E.W.F. Stirrup School
Miami, Florida

Barbara Calabro
Teacher
Compass Rose Foundation
Ft. Myers, Florida

Lucille Calvin
Teacher
Weddington Math &
Science School
Greenville, Mississippi

Patricia Carmichael
Teacher
Teasley Middle School
Canton, Georgia

Martha Cohn
Teacher
An Wang Middle School
Lowell, Massachusetts

Stu Danzinger
Supervisor
Community Consolidated
School District 59
Arlington Heights, Illinois

Esther Draper
Supervisor/Science Specialist
Belair Math Science
Magnet School
Pine Bluff, Arkansas

Sue Esser
Teacher
Loretto Elementary
Jacksonville, Florida

Dr. Richard Fairman
Teacher
Antioch University
Yellow Springs, Ohio

Joan Goldfarb
Teacher
Indialantic Elementary
Indialantic, Florida

Deborah Gomes
Teacher
A J Gomes Elementary
New Bedford, Massachusetts

Sandy Hobart
Teacher
Mims Elementary
Mims, Florida

Tom Hocker
Teacher/Science Coach
Boston Latin Academy
Dorchester, Massachusetts

Shelley Jaques
Science Supervisor
Moore Public Schools
Moore, Oklahoma

Marguerite W. Jones
Teacher
Spearman Elementary
Piedmont, South Carolina

Kelly Kenney
Teacher
Kansas City Missouri
School District
Kansas City, Missouri

Carol Kilbane
Teacher
Riverside Elementary School
Wichita, Kansas

Robert Kolenda
Teacher
Neshaminy School District
Langhorne, Pennsylvania

Karen Lynn Kruse
Teacher
St. Paul the Apostle
Yonkers, New York

Elizabeth Loures
Teacher
Point Fermin
Elementary School
San Pedro, California

Susan MacDougall
Teacher
Brick Community Primary
Learning Center
Brick, New Jersey

Jack Marine
Teacher
Raising Horizons Quest
Charter School
Philadelphia, Pennsylvania

Nicola Micozzi Jr.
Science Coordinator
Plymouth Public Schools
Plymouth, Massachusetts

Paula Monteiro
Teacher
A J Gomes Elementary
New Bedford, Massachusetts

Tracy Newallis
Teacher
Taper Avenue Elementary
San Pedro, California

Dr. Eugene Nicolo
Supervisor, Science K-12
Moorestown School District
Moorestown, New Jersey

Jeffry Pastrak
School District of Philadelphia
Philadelphia, Pennslyvania

Helen Pedigo
Teacher
Mt. Carmel Elementary
Huntsville Alabama

Becky Peltonen
Teacher
Patterson Elementary School
Panama City, Florida

Sherri Pensler
Teacher/ESOL
Claude Pepper Elementary
Miami, Florida

Virginia Rogliano
Teacher
Bridgeview Elementary
South Charleston, West
Virginia

Debbie Sanders
Teacher
Thunderbolt Elementary
Orange Park, Florida

Grethel Santamarina
Teacher
E.W.F. Stirrup School
Miami, Florida

Migdalia Schneider
Teacher/Bilingual
Lindell School
Long Beach, New York

Susan Shelly
Teacher
Bonita Springs Elementary
Bonita Springs, Florida

Peggy Terry
Teacher
Madison Elementary
South Holland, Illinois

Jane M. Thompson
Teacher
Emma Ward Elementary
Lawrenceburg, Kentucky

Martha Todd
Teacher
W. H. Rhodes Elementary
Milton, Florida

Renee Williams
Teacher
Bloomfield Schools
Central Primary
Bloomfield, New Mexico

Myra Wood
Teacher
Madison Street Academy
Ocala, Florida

Marion Zampa
Teacher
Shawnee Mission
School District
Overland Park, Kansas

Science

See learning in a whole new light

Unit A Life Science

How do plants live in their habitats?

Chapter 2 • All About Animals

How are animals different from each other?

Unit A Life Science

How do living things help each other?

Chapter 3 • How Plants and Animals Live Together

Chapter 4 • How Living Things Grow and Change

How do living things grow in different ways?

Unit B Earth Science

What are Earth's natural resources?

Chapter 6 • Earth's Weather and Seasons

How does weather change?

Unit B Earth Science

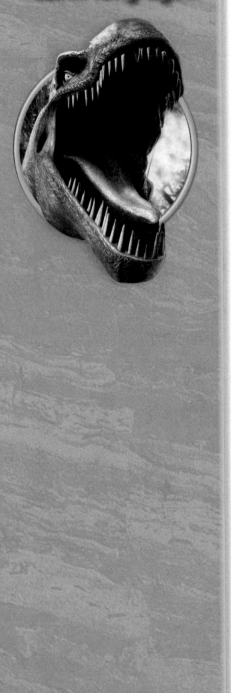

How can people learn about the Earth long ago?

Chapter 7 • Fossils and Dinosaurs

What are some properties of matter?

Chapter 9 • Energy

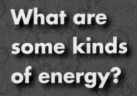

What are some kinds of energy?

Unit C Physical Science

How do forces cause objects to move?

Chapter 10 • Forces and Motion

Chapter 11 • Sound

How is sound
made?

Unit D · Space and Technology

What are some ways the Earth moves?

Chapter 12 • Earth and Space

Chapter 13 • Technology in Our World

**What are
some ways
technology
helps us?**

How to Read Science

Each chapter in your book has a page like this one. This page shows you how to use a reading skill.

Before reading
First, read the Build Background page. Next, read the How To Read Science page. Then, think about what you already know. Last, make a list of what you already know.

Target Reading Skill
Each page has a target reading skill. The target reading skill will help you understand what you read.

Real-World Connection
Each page has an example of something you will learn.

Graphic Organizer
A graphic organizer can help you think about what you learn.

How to Read Science

Reading Skills

Alike and Different

Alike means how things are the same. Different means how things are not the same.

Science Article

Worms and Snakes

Worms are long and thin. Worms do not have backbones. Worms use their bodies to crawl. Snakes are long and thin. Snakes have backbones. Snakes use their bodies to crawl.

Apply It!
Tell how a worm and a snake are alike and different. Use your **models** to help you.

Alike	Different

37

Reptiles are animals with backbones. Most reptiles have dry skin. Scales cover and protect a reptile's body. Some reptiles hatch from eggs. Snakes and turtles are two kinds of reptiles. Look at the picture of the reptile.

Amphibians are animals with backbones. Amphibians live part of their life in the water and part of their life on land. Most amphibians have smooth, wet skin. Amphibians hatch from eggs. Frogs and toads are amphibians.

☑ **Lesson Checkpoint**

1. Which kinds of animals have backbones and scales?

2. 🎯 How are an amphibian and a reptile **alike** and **different**?

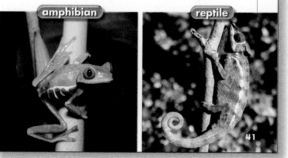

amphibian   reptile

41

Process Skills

10. **Communicate** Choose an animal in this chapter. Tell one way the animal is adapted to its environment.

🎯 **Alike and Different**

11. Tell how a spider and an insect are **alike** and **different**.

Alike	Different

🦉 **Test Prep**

Fill in the circle next to the correct answer.

12. Which kind of animal has feathers and wings?
   Ⓐ fish
   Ⓑ bird
   Ⓒ mammal
   Ⓓ amphibian

13. Writing in Science Choose an animal. Tell how the animal is adapted to its environment.

61

🎯 During reading

Use the checkpoint as you read the lesson. This will help you check how much you understand.

🎯 After reading

Think about what you have learned. Compare what you learned with the list you made before you read the chapter. Answer the questions in the Chapter Review.

Target Reading Skills

These are some target reading skills that appear in this book.

- Cause and Effect
- Alike and Different
- Put Things in Order
- Predict

- Draw Conclusions
- Picture Clues
- Important Details

Science Process Skills

Scientists use process skills to find out about things. You will use these skills when you do the activities in this book. Suppose scientists want to learn more about space. Which process skills might they use?

Space

Observe

A scientist who wants to find out more about space observes many things. You use your senses to find out about things too.

Classify

Scientists classify objects in space. You classify when you sort or group things by their properties.

Estimate and Measure

Scientists build machines to explore space. First scientists make a careful guess about the size or amount of the parts of the machine. Then they measure each part.

Infer

Scientists are always learning about space. Scientists draw a conclusion or make a guess from what they already know.

Predict
First scientists tell what they think will happen. Then they do an experiment.

Make and Use Models
Scientists might make and use models of a machine to use in space. Models show what scientists already know.

Make Definitions
Scientists use what they know to tell what something means.

Science Process Skills

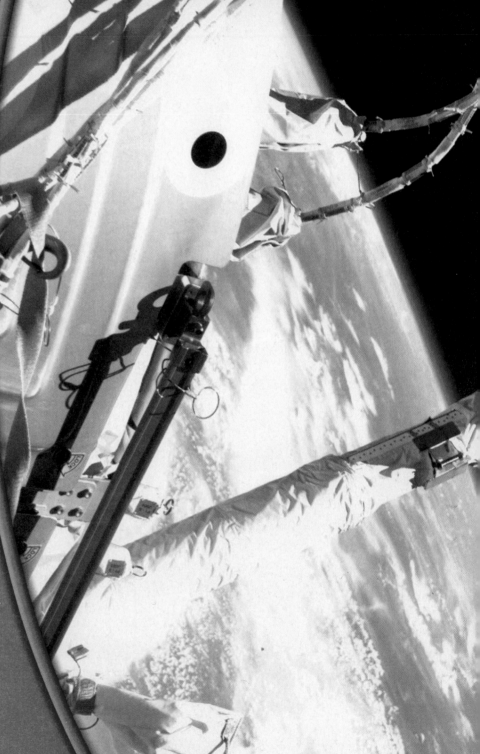

Suppose you were a scientist. You might want to learn more about space. What questions might you have? How would you use process skills to help you learn?

Make Hypotheses

Think of a question you have about space. Make a statement that you can test to answer your question.

Collect Data

Scientists record what they observe and measure. Scientists put this data into charts or graphs.

Interpret Data

Scientists use what they learn to solve problems or answer questions.

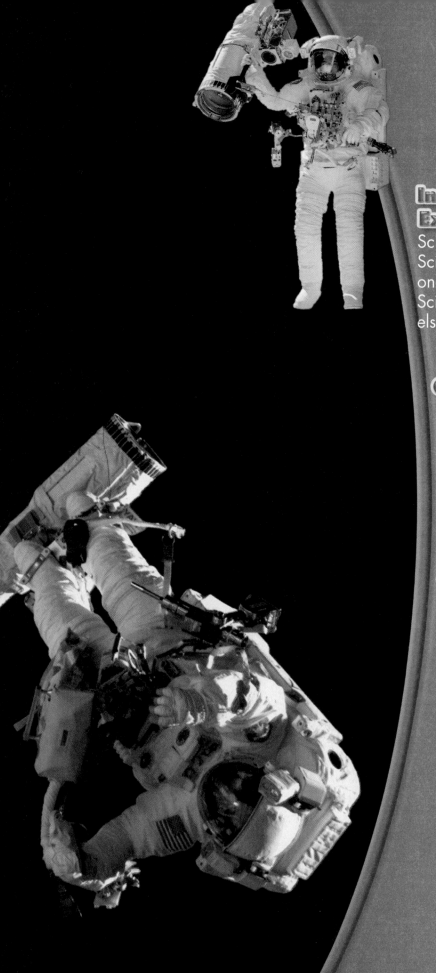

Investigate and Experiment

Scientists plan a fair test. Scientists change only one thing in their test. Scientists keep everything else the same.

Control Variables

Scientists plan and do an investigation as they study space.

Communicate

Scientists tell what they learn about space.

Using Scientific Methods

Scientific methods are ways of finding answers. Scientific methods have these steps. Sometimes scientists do the steps in a different order. Scientists do not always do all of the steps.

Ask a question.

Ask a question that you want answered.

Do seeds need water to grow?

Make your hypothesis.

Tell what you think the answer is to your question.

If seeds are watered, then they will grow.

Plan a fair test.

Change only one thing.

Keep everything else the same.

Water one pot with seeds.

no water

water

Do your test.

Test your hypothesis. Do your test more than once. See if your results are the same.

Collect and record your data.

Keep records of what you find out. Use words or drawings to help.

Tell your conclusion.

Observe the results of your test. Decide if your hypothesis is right or wrong. Tell what you decide.

Seeds need water to grow.

water

no water

Go further.

Use what you learn. Think of new questions or better ways to do a test.

Ask a Question

Make Your Hypothesis

Plan a Fair Test

Do Your Test

Collect and Record Your Data

Tell Your Conclusion

Go Further

Science Tools

Scientists use many different kinds of tools.

Safety goggles
You can use safety goggles to protect your eyes.

Hand lens
A hand lens makes objects look larger.

Clock
A clock measures time.

Magnet

You can use a magnet to see if an object is made of certain metals.

Stopwatch

A stopwatch measures how long something takes.

Ruler

You can use a ruler to measure how long something is. Most scientists use a ruler to measure length in centimeters or millimeters.

Science Tools

Meterstick

You can use a meterstick to measure how long something is too. Scientists use a meterstick to measure in meters.

Balance

A balance is used to measure the mass of objects. Mass is how much matter an object has. Most scientists measure mass in grams or kilograms.

Measuring cup

You can use a measuring cup to measure volume. Volume is how much space something takes up.

8 OZ —— 240CC
7 OZ —— 210CC
6 OZ —— 180CC
5 OZ —— 150CC
4 OZ —— 120CC
3 OZ —— 90CC
2 OZ —— 60CC
1 OZ —— 30CC

Calculator

A calculator can help you do number problems, such as adding and subtracting.

Thermometer

A thermometer measures the temperature. When the temperature gets warmer, the red line moves up. When it gets cooler, the red line moves down. Most thermometers have a Celsius and Fahrenheit scale. Most scientists use the Celsius scale.

Computer

You can learn about science at a special Internet website. Go to www.pearsonsuccessnet.com.

Safety in Science

You need to be careful when doing science activities. This page includes safety tips to remember:

- Listen to your teacher's instructions.
- Never taste or smell materials unless your teacher tells you to.
- Wear safety goggles when needed.
- Handle scissors and other equipment carefully.
- Keep your work place neat and clean.
- Clean up spills immediately.
- Tell your teacher immediately about accidents or if you see something that looks unsafe.
- Wash your hands well after every activity.

You Will Discover

- how each part of a plant helps the plant live.
- where different kinds of plants live.

Chapter 1

All About
Plants

How do plants live in their habitats?

stem

flower

nutrients

Nutrients are materials that living things need to live and grow.

roots

2

environment

leaves

adapted

prairie

Explore Do plants need water?

Materials

celery

jar

water

What to Do

1 Put celery in the jar. Look at the celery.

2 Wait 1 day. How did the celery change?

3 Put water in the jar. **Predict** what will happen to the celery.

4 Wait 1 day. How did the celery change? Why did it change?

Explain Your Results

Predict What will happen if you take the celery out of the water?

Reading Skills

TARGET SKILL Predict

Predict means to tell what you think might happen next.

Science Story

Workers plant celery seeds in little pots. When the seeds begin to grow, farmers move the young plants to fields. The farmers cut the celery when it is grown.

Apply It!

Predict what will happen to the celery next. Make a graphic organizer to help you.

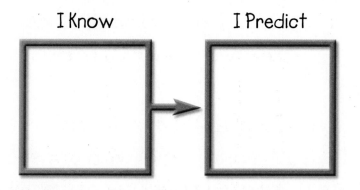

I Know

I Predict

♪ **Plants**

Sung to the tune of "Where, Oh, Where Has My Little Dog Gone?"
Lyrics by Gerri Brioso & Richard Freitas/The Dovetail Group, Inc.

Plants have roots that grow in soil,
And hold the plant in place.
The roots take in water and nutrients,
And carry them up to the stem.

What are the parts of a plant?

Plants need water, air, and sunlight. Plants need space to grow. Plants need nutrients. **Nutrients** are materials that living things need to live and grow. Many plants get nutrients from soil and water.

The parts of a plant help it get food, water, air, and sunlight.

Plant Parts

Plants have different parts. The four main parts are the roots, stem, leaves, and flowers.

Roots grow down into the soil. Roots hold the plant in place. Roots take water and nutrients from the soil to the stem.

The **stem** carries water and nutrients to the leaves. The stem holds up the plant.

Green **leaves** take in sunlight and air. They use sunlight, air, water, and nutrients to make food for the plant.

Leaves

Roots

Many plants have flowers. A **flower** makes seeds. These seeds might grow into new plants.

Flower

Stem

Seeds

✓ **Lesson Checkpoint**

1. What are the four main parts of a plant?

2. **Writing** in Science

   Write a sentence in your journal. Tell why the stem of a plant is important.

Lesson 2

How are seeds scattered?

Many new plants grow from seeds. Suppose you plant seeds. You would scatter the seeds in the soil. Scatter means to spread out. The seeds have space to grow.

Fruits cover and protect seeds. When fruits travel, the seeds inside are scattered. Some fruits are scattered by air or water. Some fruits get stuck on the fur or feathers of animals. Scattering helps carry seeds to new places where they might grow.

✓ Lesson Checkpoint

1. Name 3 ways that seeds travel.

2. **Predict** A maple tree fruit spins to the ground. It lands in an open field. What do you think might happen next?

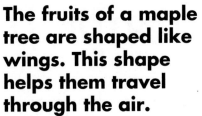

The fruits of a maple tree are shaped like wings. This shape helps them travel through the air.

The fruits of the water lily float on lakes and streams.

Burrs are fruits. Burrs travel by sticking on clothing or fur. This dog has burrs stuck to its fur.

How are plants grouped?

Plants can be grouped into two kinds. One kind of plant has flowers. The other kind of plant does not have flowers.

Plants with flowers grow in different places. Trees are plants. Some trees have flowers. The flowers form fruits that cover and protect the seeds inside.

Peach trees grow flowers. Peaches are a fruit. You can eat peaches.

Cactus plants grow in the desert. Their flowers form seeds. Some seeds fall into the sand. New cactus plants might grow.

Saguaro cactus flowers open during cool nights.

1. ✓**Checkpoint** How are plants grouped?

2. **Health** in Science Name some fruits that you can eat.

Plants Without Flowers

Not all plants have flowers. Some plants have cones. Seeds grow inside the cones. When a cone opens, the seeds fall out. Some seeds grow into new trees.

Mosses are tiny plants that do not have flowers. Mosses do not make seeds or fruits. Mosses do not have leaves, roots, or stems.

Ferns do not have flowers. Ferns do not make seeds. Ferns have leaves, roots, and stems.

✓ **Lesson Checkpoint**

1. What grows inside cones?

2. **Art** in Science Draw a forest. Label trees, mosses, and ferns.

Pine trees have cones.

Mosses often grow on wet rocks.

Some ferns live in warm, shady, wet places.

Lesson 4

How are some woodland plants adapted?

Plants live almost everywhere. A plant's **environment** is all the living and nonliving things around it.

Living things have **adapted,** or changed, to live in their environment.

Many kinds of plants grow in a woodland environment. Pine trees are adapted to live in cold weather. Pine trees have small leaves that are shaped like needles.

Pine tree leaves are adapted to keep from drying out in cold weather.

SciLinks Take It to the Net
pearsonsuccessnet.com
keyword: environment
code: g2p16

Maple tree leaves turn color in the fall.

Maple trees are adapted to live where summers are warm and winters are cold. Maple trees have large flat leaves. The maple tree loses its leaves in winter. This helps the tree keep the water it needs to live in winter.

1. ✓Checkpoint How are pine trees adapted to their environment?

2. Math in Science Find a leaf outside. Use paper clips and counters to measure it.

Plants That Live Near Water

Some plants in a woodland environment live near rivers and streams.

Plants that grow near rivers and streams are adapted to live where it is very wet.

This red plant is called a cardinal plant. The roots of a cardinal plant are adapted to get nutrients from the moist soil in a woodland.

**Cardinal
plant**

✓ **Lesson Checkpoint**

1. How is a fanwort adapted to its wet habitat?

2. **Social Studies** in Science
Look at a map. Find a river or stream in your state.

The stinging nettle has tiny, sharp hairs on its stem. The hairs protect the plant from animals that want to eat it.

The fanwort is adapted to live in water. Water can move through the thin leaves of the plant.

19

How are some prairie plants adapted?

A **prairie** is flat land with lots of grass and few trees. Many prairies have hot summers with little rain. Some prairie plants are adapted to keep water when there is not enough rain.

Goldenrod plants have stiff stems and leaves. The stems and leaves help the plants keep the water they need to live.

Goldenrod

✓ **Lesson Checkpoint**

1. How are goldenrod plants adapted?

2. **Writing in Science** Write a sentence in your **science journal.** Tell how prairie plants are different from woodland plants.

Prairie smoke has fuzz on its stems and leaves. The fuzz helps the plant keep the water it needs.

Prairie grasses have thin leaves. The leaves help the plants keep the water they need.

Lesson 6

How are some desert plants adapted?

Many deserts are sunny and hot during the day. Deserts can be cool at night. Very little rain falls in a desert environment.

Some desert plants are adapted to hold water for a long time. The desert almond has leaves that grow in different directions. Some leaves get less sunlight than others. Leaves that get less sunlight can keep the water they need to live.

Desert almond

✓Lesson Checkpoint

1. Tell about the leaves of a desert almond.

2. **Social Studies** in Science
   Find Arizona on a map. Name a desert in Arizona.

The saguaro cactus has a long, thick stem that holds water.

The octopus tree has long spines. The spines protect the plant from animals that want to eat the leaves.

How are some marsh plants adapted?

A marsh is an environment that is very wet. The soil in a marsh may not have the nutrients plants need. The plants in a marsh are adapted to get nutrients in other ways.

Cattails are plants. Cattails are adapted to grow in very wet soil. Cattails get the nutrients they need from the water.

Cattails

✔ **Lesson Checkpoint**

1. How does a sundew plant trap insects?

2. **Predict** An insect lands on the leaf of a Venus's-flytrap. Predict what will happen next.

A sundew plant gets some nutrients from insects. The plant has sticky hairs on each leaf. Insects land on a leaf and stick to the hairs.

A Venus's-flytrap also gets some nutrients from insects. An insect lands on the plant's leaves. Then the leaves snap shut.

Investigate Do plants need light?

Plants need water, air, sunlight, and nutrients to live and grow. What might happen if plants do not get light?

Materials

2 cups with grass

water

What to Do

1 Water both plants.

You can paint your cups!

2 Put one plant in sunlight.

3 Put the other plant in a dark place.

Process Skills

You **observe** when you look closely at the plants.

4 How do you think the plants will look after 1 week? **Observe** the plants every day for 1 week.

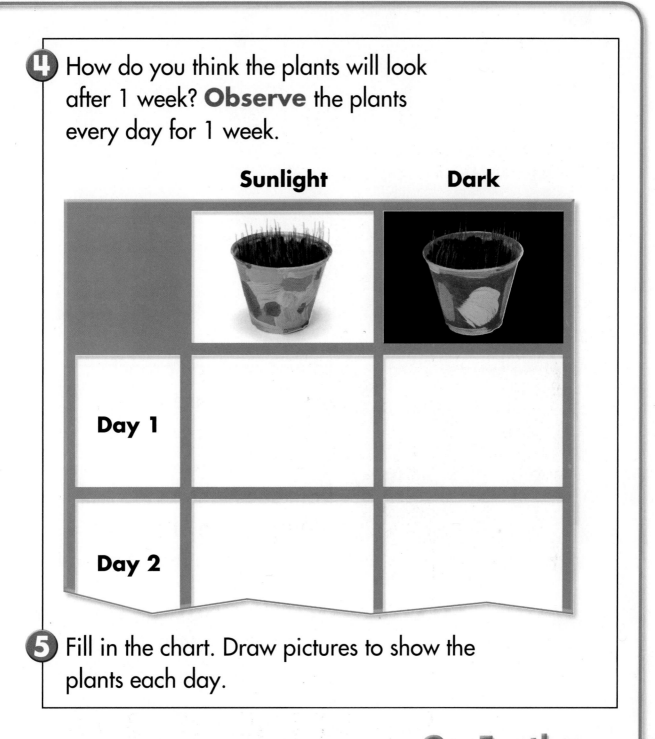

	Sunlight	Dark
Day 1		
Day 2		

5 Fill in the chart. Draw pictures to show the plants each day.

Explain Your Results
1. Which plant grew better?
2. **Infer** What will happen if a plant does not get sunlight?

Go Further
What will happen if you move the plant from the dark place to a sunny place? Try it and find out.

Leaf Patterns

Ash tree leaves

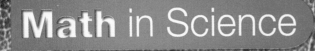

Leaves grow on branches in different patterns. Ash tree leaves grow in pairs. Two leaves grow across from each other. One leaf is on one side of a stalk. One leaf is on the other side.

Beech tree leaves grow in a different pattern. One leaf grows on one side of a stalk. Farther down, another leaf grows on the other side of the branch. This pattern repeats.

Beech tree leaves

Copy the leaf pictures below. Use what you know about leaf patterns. Predict where the next two leaves will grow. Draw two more leaves on each stalk.

Lab zone **Take-Home Activity**

Take your drawings home. Discuss what you have learned about the way leaves grow with your family.

Vocabulary

Which picture goes with each word?

1. stem
2. leaf
3. flowers
4. prairie
5. roots

What did you learn?

6. What are nutrients?
7. What is a plant's environment?
8. How is prairie smoke adapted to live on a prairie?

9. **Infer** What might happen if a plant does not get enough space to live and grow?

Predict

10. The leaves on a maple tree change color from green to red. **Predict** what will happen next.

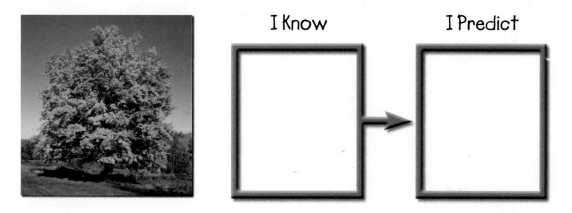

I Know

I Predict

Test Prep

Fill in the circle next to the correct answer.

11. Which part of a plant brings water up to the leaves?

Ⓐ stem

Ⓑ cone

Ⓒ roots

Ⓓ flower

12. Writing in Science Name the 4 main parts of a plant. Tell how each part helps the plant.

Mary Agnes Chase

Read Together

Mary Agnes Chase was born in 1869. She liked to collect plants when she was young. She drew pictures of the plants.

When she was older, Mary Agnes Chase became a plant scientist. She went all over the world studying plants. She kept drawing pictures of all the different plants.

Mary Agnes Chase wrote books to help other people learn about plants. Her drawings were in her books.

Mary Agnes Chase enjoyed learning about and drawing grasses.

Lab zone Take-Home Activity

Find a grass plant or other plant growing outside. Draw a picture of it. Talk to your family about your drawing.

You Will Discover

- that there are many different kinds of animals.
- how animals are adapted to different kinds of environments.

Chapter 2
All About Animals

Web Games
Take It to the Net
pearsonsuccessnet.com

online
Student Edition
pearsonsuccessnet.com

How are animals different from each other?

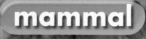
mammal

bird

fish gills

Chapter 2 Vocabulary

reptile

amphibian

camouflage

insect

35

Explore How are worms and snakes alike and different?

Materials

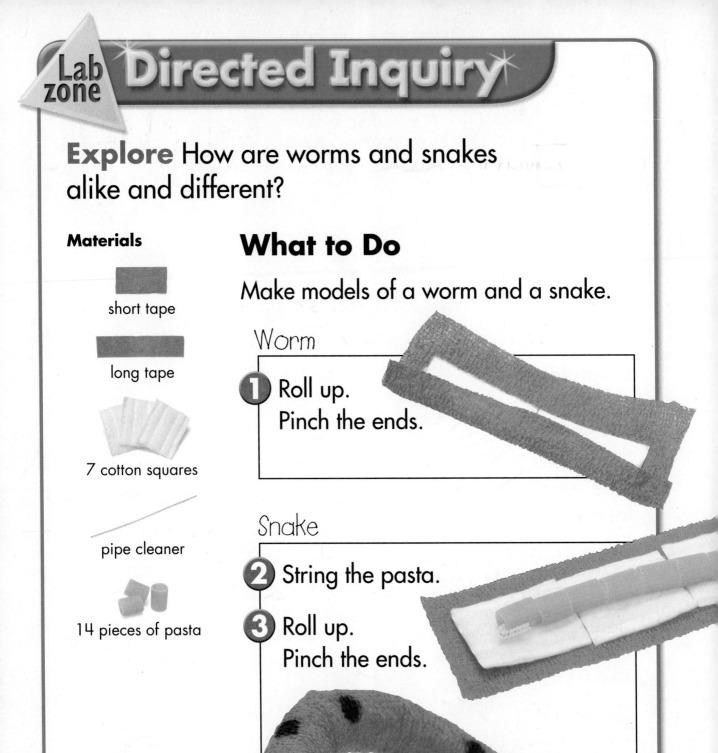

short tape

long tape

7 cotton squares

pipe cleaner

14 pieces of pasta

What to Do

Make models of a worm and a snake.

Worm

1 Roll up.
Pinch the ends.

Snake

2 String the pasta.

3 Roll up.
Pinch the ends.

Process Skills

Models show how animals are alike and different.

Explain Your Results

Feel the **models**. Tell about them.

Reading Skills

Alike and Different

Alike means how things are the same.
Different means how things are not the same.

Science Article

Worms and Snakes

Worms are long and thin. Worms do not have backbones. Worms use their bodies to crawl. Snakes are long and thin. Snakes have backbones. Snakes use their bodies to crawl.

Apply It!

Tell how a worm and a snake are alike and different. Use your **models** to help you.

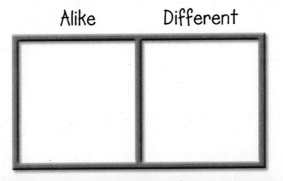

Alike	Different

What Has Backbones?

Sung to the tune of "There's a Hole In The Bucket"
Lyrics by Gerri Brioso & Richard Freitas/The Dovetail Group, Inc.

There are animals with backbones,

Like mammals.

Yes, mammals.

Dogs and cats,

Skunks and chipmunks,

All have backbones.

What are some animals with backbones?

There are many different kinds of animals. One main group of animals has backbones.

Bones help give an animal shape. Bones can help an animal move. Bones can help protect some body parts of animals.

A skunk has a backbone.

Animals with Backbones

Mammals are animals with backbones.
A mammal usually has hair or fur on its body.
Young mammals get milk from their mother.
Dogs and cats are two kinds of mammals.
The chipmunk in the picture is a mammal.

Birds are animals with backbones. Birds have feathers and wings. Birds hatch from eggs.

Fish are animals with backbones. Fish live in water. Most fish are covered with scales. Fish have fins. Most fish hatch from eggs.

mammal

bird

fish

40

Reptiles are animals with backbones. Most reptiles have dry skin. Scales cover and protect a reptile's body. Some reptiles hatch from eggs. Snakes and turtles are two kinds of reptiles.

Amphibians are animals with backbones. Amphibians live part of their life in the water and part of their life on land. Most amphibians have smooth, wet skin. Amphibians hatch from eggs. Frogs and toads are amphibians.

✓ **Lesson Checkpoint**

1. Which kinds of animals have backbones and scales?

2. 🎯 How are an amphibian and a reptile **alike** and **different?**

reptile

amphibian

41

Lesson 2

What are some ways mammals are adapted?

Mammals live almost everywhere in the world. Like plants, mammals have adapted to live in their environment. An animal's environment is all the living and nonliving things around it.

Like many animals, mule deer are adapted to their environment by camouflage. **Camouflage** is a color or shape that makes a plant or animal hard to see.

The mule deer's fur is brown in summer.

In winter, the mule deer's fur turns color. The deer is harder to see in the snow.

summer

winter

A flying squirrel is adapted to glide from tree to tree.

A chipmunk sleeps for part of the winter.

Some animals are adapted to act in ways that help them live. Chipmunks store some of the food they find in the summer. They sleep for part of the winter. Chipmunks eat some of the food they store every time they wake up.

✓ **Lesson Checkpoint**

1. How does a mule deer's fur change in winter?

2. **Art** in Science Draw a picture of a mammal that you have seen.

What are some ways birds are adapted?

Many birds are adapted to fly. Wings and feathers help birds fly.

This bird is called a nightjar.

The nightjar lives in fields. Its feathers look like the ground. This camouflage helps the bird hide from animals that might eat it.

Hmmm!
A hummingbird's beak is adapted. A hummingbird uses its beak to drink liquid from flowers.

Most penguins live where it is very cold.

A penguin's top feathers are waterproof. These feathers help keep the penguin dry. Tiny feathers below the top feathers trap air. The trapped air helps keep the penguin warm.

Penguins do not fly. Their wings are adapted for swimming.

✓ Lesson Checkpoint

1. How does camouflage protect the nightjar?

2. 🎯 How are hummingbirds and penguins **alike?** How are they **different?**

45

What are some ways fish are adapted?

Fish are adapted to life in the water. Fish have gills. **Gills** are body parts that help fish get oxygen from the water. Fish have fins to help them swim.

This porcupine fish is adapted to protect itself. The porcupine fish can make itself big. Sharp spikes stick out from its body when it is big.

Gill   Fin

This tiny porcupine fish can become very big.

Changing shape protects the porcupine fish.

Many catfish live in lakes and rivers. Catfish can swim deep in the water where it is dark. Catfish have feelers that look like whiskers. Feelers help catfish find food.

Long feelers help a catfish find food.

This stingray uses the sharp spike on its tail to protect itself.

✓ Lesson Checkpoint

1. How do porcupine fish protect themselves?

2. Math in Science Some catfish are only 10 centimeters long. Use a ruler. Draw a line 10 centimeters long. Find something in your classroom that is the same length.

What are some ways reptiles are adapted?

Reptiles are adapted to changes in air temperature. A reptile's body is cold when the air is cold. A reptile's body is warm when the air is warm. Reptiles can move quickly when they are warm.

Zap!

A chameleon has a long tongue. The chameleon has a sticky ball at the end of its tongue. Food sticks to this ball.

Open wide!

This snake's mouth is adapted to open very wide. This snake can swallow its food whole.

A desert iguana is adapted to live in the hot, sunny desert. Dark colors get hot in the sun. Light colors stay cooler in the sun. The light skin helps the desert iguana keep cool.

desert iguana

☑ **Lesson Checkpoint**

1. How is a desert iguana adapted to live in its environment?

2. **Writing in Science** Tell one way some snakes are adapted to get food.

What are some ways amphibians are adapted?

Most amphibians begin their life in the water. Many amphibians move to the land when they are grown. Frogs are amphibians. Frogs often live near water. Smooth, wet skin helps frogs live in moist environments.

These tree frogs have bright red eyes. Other animals want to eat the frogs. The frogs' eyes help scare these animals away.

Toads are amphibians. Toads begin their life in water. Toads move to the land when they are grown. Toads dig deep into the ground when it is very hot. They look for food at night.

Most toads have dry, rough skin.

✔ **Lesson Checkpoint**

1. Name one way a toad and a frog are different.

2. **Writing** in Science Tell how bright red eyes can help a tree frog.

Lesson 7

What are some animals without backbones?

One main group of animals has backbones. Another main group of animals does not have backbones. Most kinds of animals do not have bones.

Insects are animals that do not have bones. Insects have three body parts. The body parts are the head, the thorax, and the abdomen. Insects have six legs. Antennae help some insects feel, smell, hear, and taste.

Abdomen

This insect is called a walking stick. Camouflage makes the insect hard to see on a plant.

Some kinds of honeypot ants are adapted to store water and food in their abdomens.

Thorax

A diving beetle's legs are adapted. Its hairy legs help the beetle swim.

Antennae

Head

1. ✓ **Checkpoint** How is the diving beetle adapted to life in water?

2. **Technology** in Science Tell about inventions that help people move in water.

Other Animals Without Backbones

An octopus lives in the ocean. An octopus is an animal without a backbone.

An octopus is adapted to find and catch food. An octopus has good eyesight. Its eyesight helps it find food. The suction cups on its arms help the octopus hold its food.

An octopus has 8 arms.

Spiders are animals without backbones. Spiders have eight legs. Spiders are adapted to spin webs. The webs trap insects that spiders eat.

This spider builds a web to trap insects.

✔ **Lesson Checkpoint**

1. Tell how the octopus is adapted to find food.

2. **Math in Science** A spider has 8 legs. How many legs will 2 spiders have in all? Write a number sentence to show your answer.

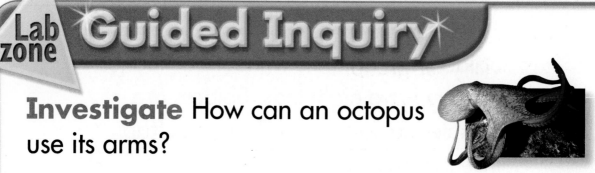
Investigate How can an octopus use its arms?

An octopus has suction cups on its 8 arms. It can use its arms to pick things up. Billye the octopus uses its arms to solve a problem. Billye can open a jar to get a fish inside.

Materials

scissors

fish

jar

8 suction cups

What to Do

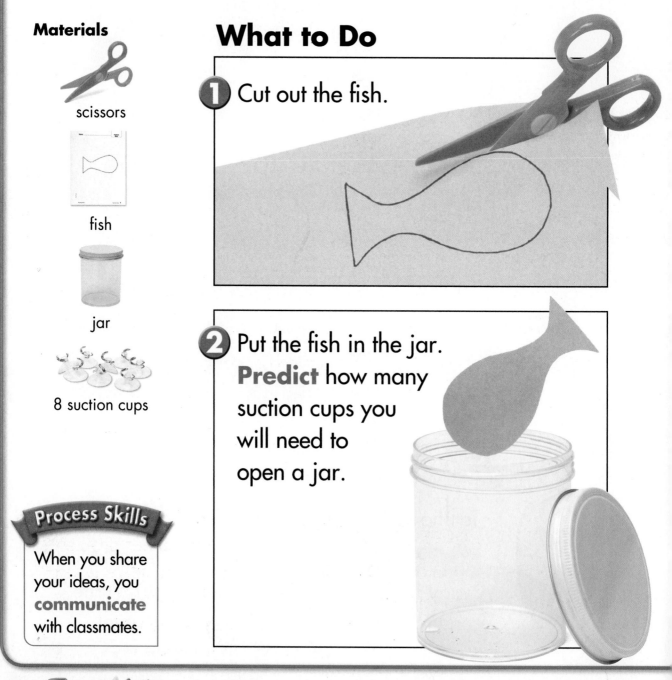

1 Cut out the fish.

2 Put the fish in the jar. **Predict** how many suction cups you will need to open a jar.

3 Work with your group. Take turns. Try to open the jar with suction cups. Where should you put them?

4 How many suction cups did you predict? How many did you use?

How many suction cups will open a jar?								
Predict								
Test								

1   2   3   4   5   6   7   8

Number of Suction Cups

Explain Your Results
Communicate Tell how you used the suction cups.

Go Further

What other problems can you solve using suction cups? Try to solve the problems!

Math in Science

Sorting Animals

Sort these animals into 2 groups. One group has animals with backbones. Count the number of animals with backbones. The other group has animals without backbones. Count the number of animals without backbones.

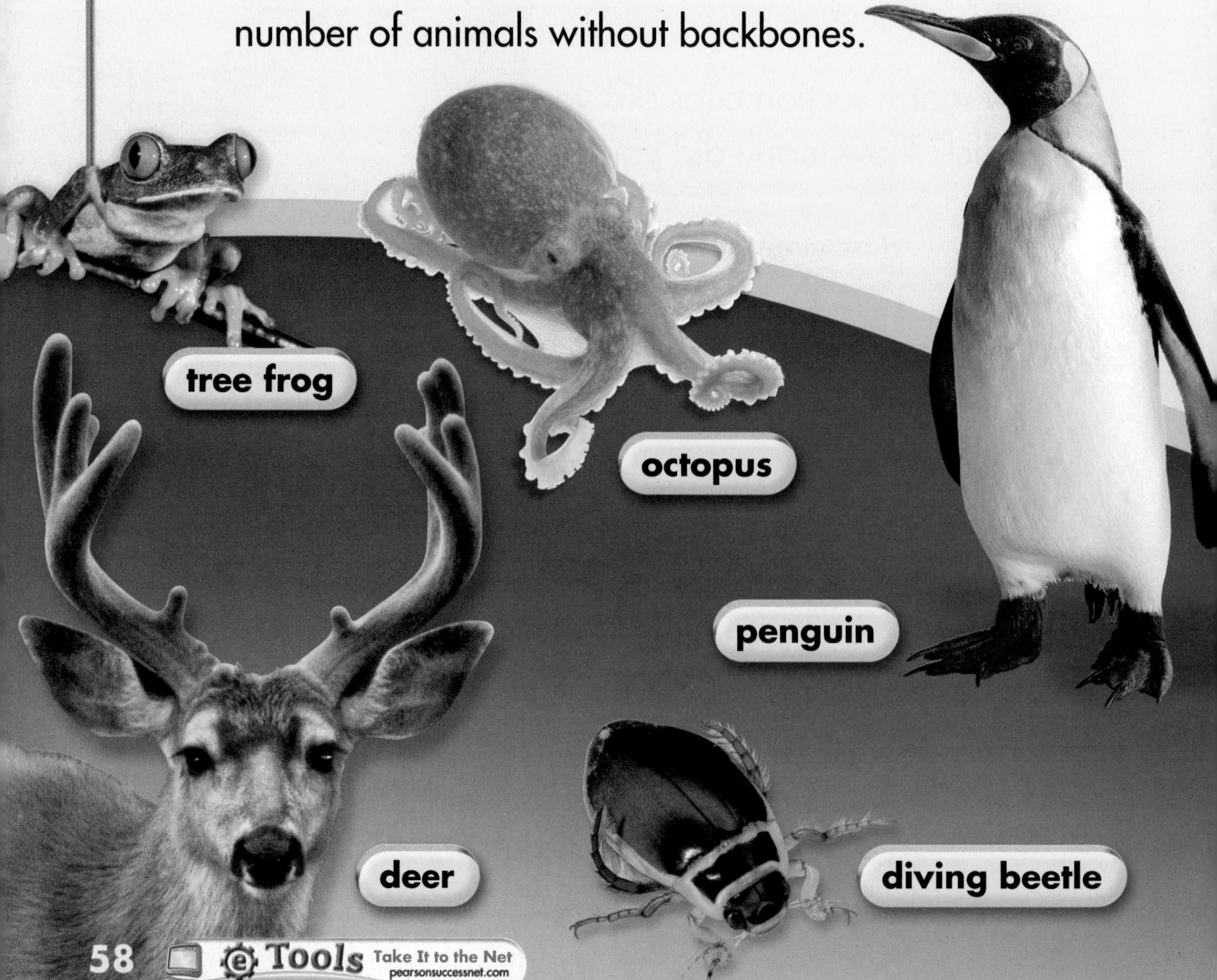

tree frog
octopus
penguin
deer
diving beetle

Make a graph like this one. Color in your graph to show the number of animals in each group.

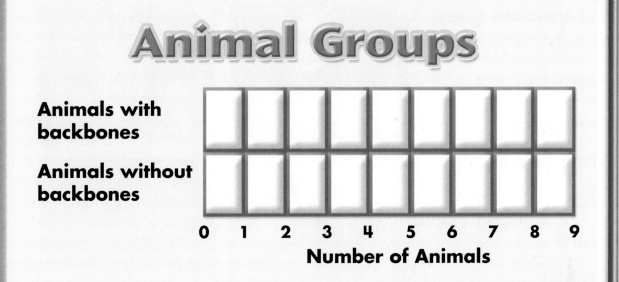

Animal Groups

Animals with backbones

Animals without backbones

0 1 2 3 4 5 6 7 8 9

Number of Animals

1. Which group has the most animals?
2. Which group has the fewest animals?

snake

porcupine fish

Lab zone **Take-Home Activity**

Take a nature walk. List all of the animals you see. Sort the animals into groups.

Vocabulary

Which picture goes with each word?

1. insect
2. mammal
3. amphibian
4. fish
5. bird
6. reptile

What did you learn?

7. How do fish use gills?

8. How does camouflage help protect animals?

9. Name 2 kinds of animals with backbones. Name 2 kinds of animals without backbones.

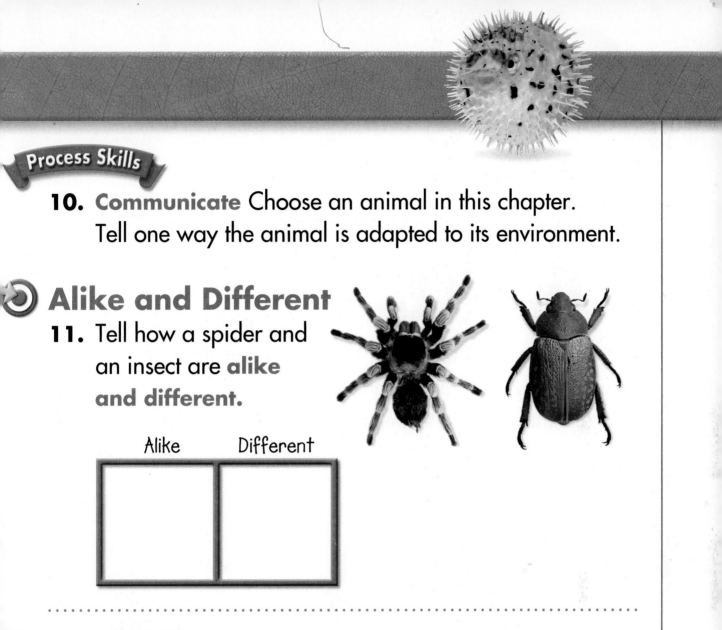

10. Communicate Choose an animal in this chapter. Tell one way the animal is adapted to its environment.

Alike and Different

11. Tell how a spider and an insect are **alike and different.**

Alike	Different

Test Prep

Fill in the circle next to the correct answer.

12. Which kind of animal has feathers and wings?

Ⓐ fish

Ⓑ bird

Ⓒ mammal

Ⓓ amphibian

13. Writing in Science Choose an animal. Tell how the animal is adapted to its environment.

Life Along the Ice

Scientists working with NASA use satellites to study animals and their environments. Scientists use satellites to learn about penguins that live near Antarctica.

Antarctica is very cold. Most of the ocean water near Antarctica is full of ice. The wind blows holes in the ice. Plants called algae can grow in the holes in the ice. Tiny animals called krill eat the algae. Penguins eat krill.

Scientists have learned that when there are more algae, there are more krill. When there are more krill, there are more penguins. When there are fewer krill, there are fewer penguins.

Krill

Satellites send information about the ocean back to Earth.

Lab zone **Take-Home Activity**

Draw a picture of a penguin. Tell your family how scientists learn about the ocean. Tell them how the amount of krill affects the number of penguins.

Wildlife Rehabilitator

Read Together

What happens when animals that live in forests or oceans are hurt? Are there ways people can help?

Wildlife rehabilitators are people that help hurt or sick animals. They know what animals need to live in their environment. A wildlife rehabilitator can even teach young animals how to hunt for food.

Wildlife rehabilitators know that it is important that animals get the care they need to survive.

A wildlife rehabilitator saved this sea turtle.

Lab zone Take-Home Activity

Write about what it would be like to be a wildlife rehabilitator. What kinds of animals would you like to help?

You Will Discover

- what plants and animals need.
- how animals depend on plants and other animals.

Chapter 3

How Plants and Animals Live Together

online
Student Edition
pearsonsuccessnet.com

65

How do living things help each other?

producer

consumer

predator

prey

Chapter 3 Vocabulary

food web

Sun

food chain

67

Explore What does yeast need to grow?

Yeast are tiny living things.
They cannot make their own food.
They must get food from where they live.

Be careful! Don't slip!
Clean up spills.

Materials

cup with yeast

cup with warm water

cup with sugar

spoon

You can **infer** from what you observe with your senses.

What to Do

1 Put water in the cup with yeast.

2 Add sugar and stir. Watch the yeast.

Look at the tiny bubbles!

3 **Estimate** How long did it take to see tiny bubbles?

Explain Your Results

Infer What made the yeast change?

 **Cause and Effect**

A cause is why something happens.
An effect is what happens.

Science Activity

Yeast is added to bread dough. The yeast causes air bubbles to form in the bread dough. The air bubbles make the bread dough rise.

Apply It!

Infer What would happen to the bread dough without the yeast?

Cause   Effect

Good Partners

Sung to the tune of "Frere Jacques"
Lyrics by Gerri Brioso & Richard Freitas/The Dovetail Group, Inc.

Plants and animals
Are good partners.
Yes they are.
Yes they are.

What do plants and animals need?

You learned that plants need air, water, sunlight, nutrients, and space to grow. Most green plants are producers. A **producer** is a living thing that can make its own food.

Animals need air, water, shelter, and space to live. Animals need food. Animals are consumers. A **consumer** cannot make its own food. Consumers get food from their habitat.

These giraffes are consumers.

Different Needs

Many plants and animals live together in a habitat. Plants and animals depend on each other and their habitat to meet their needs.

Large animals often need a lot of food, water, and space. Large animals need a large shelter. Small animals often do not need as much to eat and drink as large animals. Small animals can live in small spaces.

These plants and animals live in the same habitat.

These animals both need water. Which animal do you think needs more water?

Sometimes a habitat does not have enough food for all of the animals that live there. When this happens, some of the animals might die.

✓ **Lesson Checkpoint**

1. What do all animals need?

2. 🎯 **Cause and Effect** What might happen if there is not enough food for all of the animals in a habitat?

Lesson 2

How do plants and animals get food in a grassland?

All living things need food. Most plants make food. Some animals eat plants. Other animals eat those animals. This is called a **food chain.**

Food chains start with the Sun. Plants use energy from the Sun to make food. Animals get energy from the food they eat. Look at the pictures of the food chain. Energy passes from sunlight to the mountain lion.

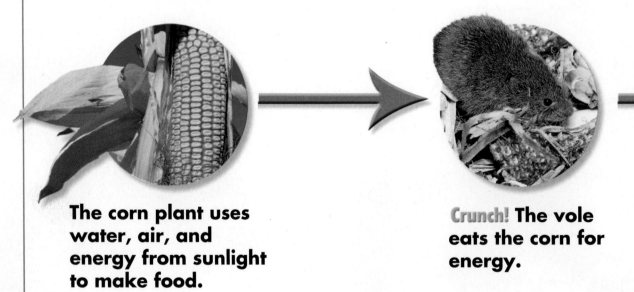

The corn plant uses water, air, and energy from sunlight to make food.

Crunch! The vole eats the corn for energy.

All food chains have predators and prey. A **predator** is an animal that catches and eats another animal. **Prey** is an animal that is caught and eaten. Look at the animals in the food chain. The coyote and mountain lion are predators. Which animals are their prey?

1. ✔Checkpoint Give an example of a predator and its prey.

2. Art in Science Draw a picture of this grassland food chain. Label your picture.

Pounce! **The mountain lion catches and eats the coyote.**

Gulp! **The coyote eats the vole. The vole is the coyote's prey.**

A Food Web in a Grassland

Habitats usually have more than one food chain. The food chains in a habitat make up a **food web.** The plants and animals in a food web need each other for energy.

raccoon

corn plant

vole

fox

These pages show a food web in a grassland. Energy passes from sunlight to the corn. Use your finger to trace how energy moves from the corn to the vole to the fox. This is one food chain. What other food chains can you find on these two pages?

hawk

coyote

mountain lion

✔ Lesson Checkpoint

1. Describe a food web.

2. **Math** in Science How many animals in this food web eat the corn? How many animals eat the vole? How many more animals eat the vole than the corn? Write a number sentence.

How do plants and animals get food in an ocean?

An ocean has food chains and food webs too. Many different plants and animals live in an ocean. The pictures on these pages show an ocean food chain.

Kelp grows in an ocean. Kelp uses energy from sunlight to make food.

Sea urchins eat kelp.

Crunch! A sea star eats the sea urchin.

Remember that energy is passed through each step in a food chain. Trace how energy in this food chain passes from the Sun to the sea otter.

1. ✓Checkpoint Where does a sea otter get energy?

2. Writing in Science Write 2 or 3 sentences. Tell how energy moves through this food chain.

Chomp! The sea otter eats the sea star. The sea otter gets the energy it needs from the sea star.

A Food Web in an Ocean

Look at this simple ocean food web. Energy passes from sunlight to the kelp. Use your finger to trace the food chains. How many food chains can you count?

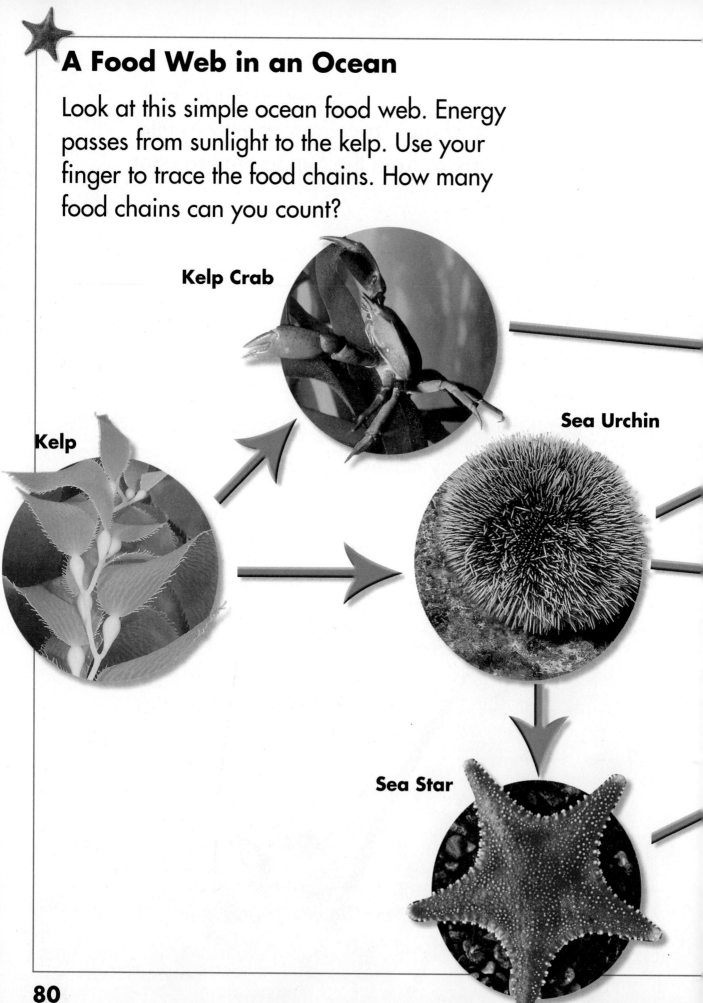

Kelp Crab

Sea Urchin

Kelp

Sea Star

Sea Otter

Orca

Sea Gull

✔ **Lesson Checkpoint**

1. What eats kelp in this food web?

2. **Writing in Science** Write one sentence in your journal. Describe one food chain in this ocean food web.

Lesson 4

What can cause a food web to change?

Many things can cause changes in a food web. Some changes may make it hard for plants and animals to survive. Parts of the food web may be harmed or even die.

This ship had an accident. Oil spilled from the ship into the ocean.

People can cause a food web to change. The picture shows an oil spill. Many plants and animals were covered with oil.

People washed the oil off of this otter's fur.

People worked together to wash the oil off the animals. People helped to clean the water. People made the water safe again for the plants and animals that live there.

✓ **Lesson Checkpoint**

1. How did people help after the oil spill?

2. **Cause and Effect** What is one effect of an oil spill?

How do plants and animals help each other?

Sometimes plants and animals help each other. Some animals get shelter from plants. These ants live inside an acacia plant. The ants protect the acacia plant from animals that might eat it.

If other animals try to eat this plant, the ants will bite them on the nose!

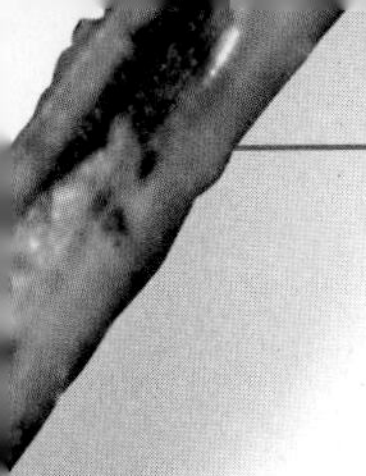

These cardinal fish stay close to the sea urchin.

cardinal fish

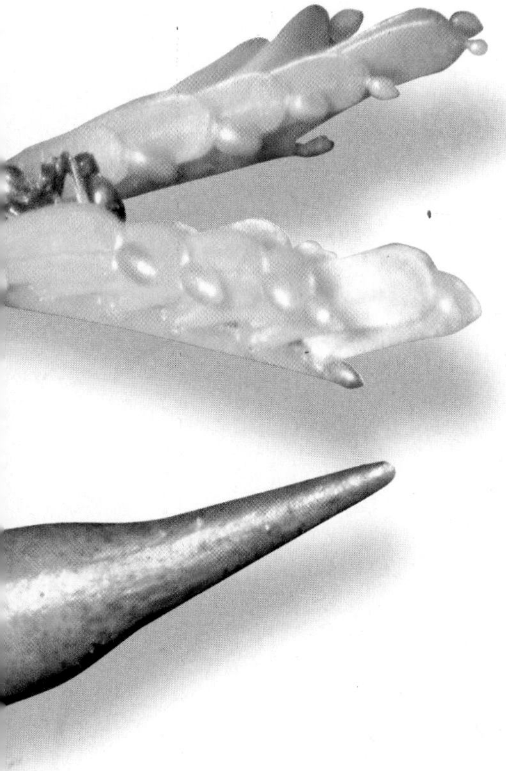

Some animals get protection from other animals. Find the cardinal fish in the picture above. Cardinal fish live near sea urchins. The sharp spines of the sea urchin protect the fish. The fish do not help or hurt the sea urchin.

1. ✓Checkpoint How do ants protect an acacia plant?

2. Social Studies in Science Acacia plants live in Costa Rica. Find Costa Rica on a map. You can find it south of Florida.

Building Nests

Some animals depend on plants and other animals to build nests. Some animals use parts of plants. Some animals use feathers or fur from other animals to build their nests.

Look at the picture of the squirrel's nest. Twigs and leaves are on the outside of the nest. Dried grass, bark, feathers, and wool are on the inside of the nest.

The masked weaver makes a nest from plant parts.

Some owls that live in the desert build their nests in a cactus.

1. ✓ **Checkpoint** What animal parts does the squirrel use to make its nest?

2. **Writing in Science** Write 2 or 3 sentences in your **science journal.** Tell what you learned about animals that build nests.

Animals Need Each Other

Animals need each other for many reasons. The remora fish in the picture below takes a ride with a blue shark. When the shark eats, the remora fish eats the leftovers! The remora does not hurt or help the shark.

The big blue shark scares predators away from the little remora.

A bird called an egret sits on top of a rhinoceros. The egret eats flies that might hurt the rhino.

Boxer crabs can hold an anemone in each claw. They use the anemones to sting predators. An anemone is a sea animal.

✓Lesson Checkpoint

1. How does a shark help a remora fish?

2. Math in Science Which is the best estimate of the weight of a rhinoceros: 35 pounds or 3,500 pounds?

Investigate How can you model a food web?

Many different living things make up a food web. All of the animals you see are part of a food web.

Materials

food web cards

tape

yarn

crayons or markers

Process Skills

When you act something out, you **model** it.

What to Do

1 Choose a card. Tape it on your shirt. Stand in a circle with your group.

2 Look for living things that you eat or that eat you. Toss the ball of yarn to one of them.

3 Take turns until everyone is connected. Lay down the yarn and the cards.

4 Draw your food web and write the names of the living things.

My Food Web

Explain Your Results

1. **Infer** What do the web lines mean?
2. How did you **model** a real food web?

Begin to model the food web.

Go Further

How could you model a grassland food web? Make a plan and try it.

Measuring Length

hawk

These animals are from this chapter. They are some of the predators and prey in a grassland food web.

fox

raccoon

vole

 Tools Take It to the Net
pearsonsuccessnet.com

Read the table. Find out how long some of the animals can grow to be.

Animal	Length in cm
Raccoon	100 cm
Vole	20 cm
Fox	80 cm
Hawk	60 cm

1. Which animal is the shortest?

2. Which animal is the longest?

3. How much longer is the fox than the vole?

4. Put the animals in order from shortest to longest.

Lab zone **Take-Home Activity**

Use a ruler. Find objects at home that match the length of each animal in the table. List the objects. Share your list with your family.

Vocabulary

Which picture goes with each word?

1. producer
2. consumer
3. food chain

A

B

C

What did you learn?

4. What do all animals need to live?

5. Name a predator from this chapter. What is its prey?

6. What are some ways animals help each other?

7. Infer What would happen to an ocean food web if there were no more kelp?

Cause and Effect

8. Read the captions.

It rained all day in this forest.

The mountain lion found shelter from the rain in a cave.

What **caused** the mountain lion to go into the cave?

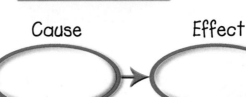

Cause   Effect

Test Prep

Fill in the circle next to the correct answer.

9. Which animal finds shelter in an acacia plant?

Ⓐ masked weaver

Ⓑ egret

Ⓒ cardinal fish

Ⓓ ant

10. Writing in Science Describe a food chain from the chapter. Tell how energy passes through it.

Farmer

Read Together

Farmers have an important job! Some farmers work on farms that grow grains, fruits, and vegetables for food. Some farmers raise animals that give people milk, eggs, and meat.

When fruits and vegetables are ready, farmers pick them. They ship the fruits and vegetables off to factories or markets. Farmers milk cows. Farmers gather eggs from chickens. Many people depend on farmers for food.

Lab zone Take-Home Activity

Draw a picture of plants and animals on a farm. Tell how a farmer cares for the plants and animals in your picture.

You Will Discover

- ways that living things are like their parents.
- how plants and animals change as they grow.

Chapter 4

How Living Things Grow and Change

How do living things grow in different ways?

life cycle

nymph

seed coat

germinate

Germinate means to begin to grow into a young plant.

seedling

Explore Which hand do different children use to write?

Materials

paper

crayon

scissors

tape

chart paper

What to Do

1 Trace the hand you use to write.

2 Write your name in the middle. Cut out the hand.

3 **Collect data** Tape your hand to the graph.

Be careful!

Scissors are sharp!

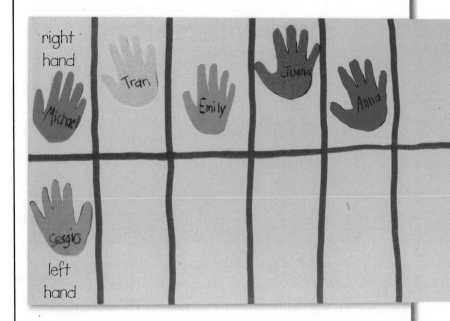

right hand

Tran

Emily

Juana

Anna

Michael

Sergio

left hand

Explain Your Results
Infer What does the graph show?

Reading Skills

TARGET SKILL Infer

Infer means to use what you know to answer a question.

Science Article

Carol is right-handed. She uses her right hand for writing and to drink from a glass. She uses both hands to button her coat. Ben is left-handed.

Apply It!

Infer Which hand do you think Ben would use to cut paper or throw a ball?

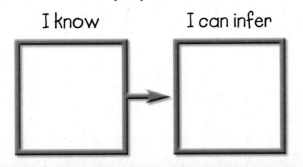

I know   I can infer

Hi Little Turtle!

Sung to the tune of "Itsy Bitsy Spider"
Lyrics by Gerri Brioso & Richard Freitas/The Dovetail Group, Inc.

Look at the sea turtle coming from the sea.

Crawling on the sand, looking right at me.

Hey, little sea turtle, I would like to know,

How did you start out and how did you grow?

Science Songs

How do sea turtles grow and change?

Living things need food and water. Living things grow and change. Living things can be parents. Plants and animals are living things.

The sea turtle is an animal. You will learn how a sea turtle grows and changes.

This toy turtle is a nonliving thing. It does not need food and water. It cannot grow and change. It cannot be a parent.

Sea Turtle Eggs

A sea turtle lives in the ocean. A sea turtle crawls onto a beach to lay eggs. A sea turtle uses its flippers to dig a hole in the sand. It lays eggs in the hole. Then the sea turtle covers the eggs with sand.

Sea turtles can lay many eggs at one time.

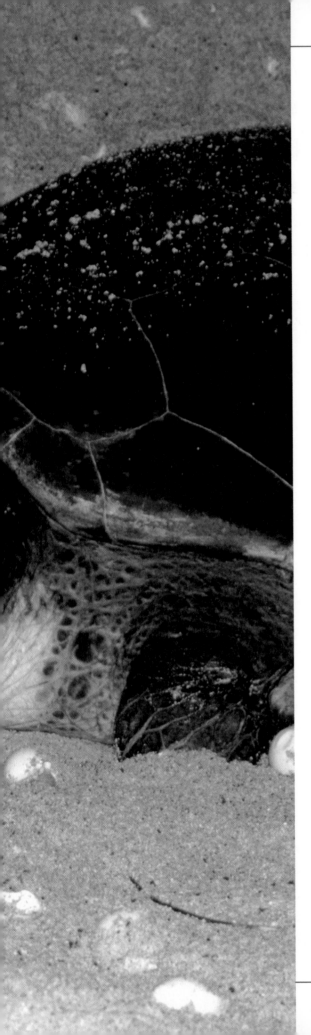

The eggs lay in the sand for about two months. Then the eggs are ready to hatch.

Baby turtles have a special tooth. The tooth helps them break open the egg's shell. Later, the tooth falls out.

A baby sea turtle hatches from its egg.

1. ✔Checkpoint How do baby sea turtles get out of the egg?

2. Math in Science Suppose 3 sea turtles each laid 100 eggs. How many eggs were laid all together?

The Life Cycle of a Sea Turtle

The way a living thing grows and changes is called its **life cycle.** Follow the arrows to see the life cycle of a sea turtle.

The sea turtle starts life as an egg.

A young sea turtle comes out of the egg. Young sea turtles look like their parents.

One day, the sea turtle may have young of its own. A new life cycle begins.

✓ Lesson Checkpoint

1. How do sea turtles start life?

2. **Social Studies** in Science Look at a map of the United States. Find some places where sea turtles might lay eggs.

What is the life cycle of a dragonfly?

The life cycles of insects are different from the life cycles of other animals. Many young insects are called **nymphs.** Nymphs look a lot like their parents, but their wings are still growing. Nymphs shed their outside covering many times as they grow.

Dragonflies often lay eggs in the water.

A nymph hatches from the dragonfly egg. First, the nymph lives in the water. Then, the nymph crawls to the land.

The nymph has shed its covering one last time. Now it is an adult dragonfly with wings to fly. It may lay eggs.

1. Tell the stages of a dragonfly life cycle in order.

2. **Infer** Why doesn't a nymph need wings?

Lesson 3

What is the life cycle of a horse?

A horse is a mammal. Most young mammals grow inside their mothers. Young mammals drink milk from their mother.

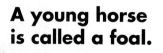

A young horse is called a foal.

The foal grows and grows. It looks like its parents.

The foal has become an adult horse. The adult horse is old enough to have foals of its own.

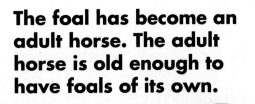

✓ Lesson Checkpoint

1. **Infer** What is food for a foal?

2. Writing in Science Tell what you know about the life cycle of a horse.

How are young animals like their parents?

Young animals often look like their parents in shape and color. Yet some young animals look different from their parents.

Young penguins are covered with fuzzy down feathers. The feathers become white and black as the penguin grows.

These kittens all have the same parents. Yet they look different from each other.

Giraffes have brown spots. Each giraffe has its own pattern of spots. No two patterns are the same.

The spots on the adult giraffe are darker than the spots on its young.

✓ Lesson Checkpoint

1. How are young penguins different from their parents?

2. **Writing** in Science Tell how you think the kittens are like their parents.

Lesson 5

What is the life cycle of a bean plant?

Most plants grow from seeds. A seed has a hard outer covering called a **seed coat.** A seed coat protects the seed.

Each seed contains a tiny plant and stored food. The tiny plant uses the stored food as it grows. A seed that gets enough water and air may **germinate,** or begin to grow. Roots from the germinated seed grow down into the ground. A stem grows up. A seedling grows out of the ground. A **seedling** is a young plant.

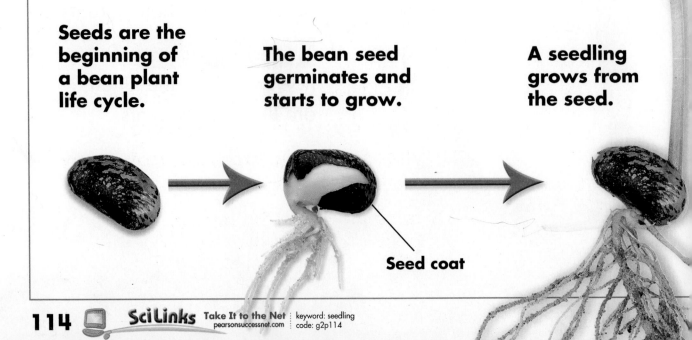

Seeds are the beginning of a bean plant life cycle.

The bean seed germinates and starts to grow.

A seedling grows from the seed.

Seed coat

SciLinks **Take It to the Net** pearsonsuccessnet.com | keyword: seedling code: g2p114

The plant continues to grow. The flowers on an adult plant make seeds. Some seeds from an adult plant will grow into new plants.

The plant continues to grow and change. It becomes an adult.

✓**Lesson Checkpoint**

1. How does a seed coat help a seed?

2. **Math** in Science A farmer plants 5 rows of bean plants. There are 10 bean plants in each row. How many bean plants did the farmer plant in all? Skip count to find the answer.

How are young plants like their parents?

Young plants are usually like the parent plant in color and shape. Young plants can be different from the parent plant in some ways too.

A young saguaro cactus has the same shape as an adult. It has the same color as an adult.

An adult saguaro cactus has arms.

A young saguaro cactus does not have arms.

These flowers are called foxgloves. Foxgloves grow leaves during their first year of life. They grow flowers during their second year of life. Look at the picture. The foxglove flowers all have the same shape. The foxglove flowers have different colors.

✓ **Lesson Checkpoint**

1. How are the foxgloves alike and different?

2. **Art** in Science Draw a young saguaro cactus and an old saguaro cactus. Write how they are different.

How do people grow and change?

People are alike in some ways. All people change as they grow. You used to be a baby. You are a child now. You have lost some of your first teeth. You have grown taller. What are some other ways you have changed?

This boy has changed since he was a baby. Now he can read and talk.

You will keep changing as you get older. You will get taller. You will become a teenager. Later, you will become an adult. Adults keep changing too. Adults do not grow taller. An adult's skin will begin to wrinkle. The color of an adult's hair may change to gray or white.

The members of this family will keep changing.

1. ✓Checkpoint What is one way all people are alike?

2. What are some ways people grow and change?

How People Are Different

People are different in some ways too.
Some people are short. Some people
are tall. Some people have brown eyes.
Some people have blue eyes. People have
different hair colors. People have different
skin colors.

Look at the many ways these children are different.

Children in the same family might look like each other. They might look different from each other too. How might children in the same family look alike? How might they look different?

Parents and their children may look alike in some ways. They may look different in other ways. Look at the family in the picture on this page. How are the children like their parents? How are they different?

People in a family do not look exactly alike.

✔️ Lesson Checkpoint

1. What are some ways people can be different from each other?

2. 🎯 **Infer** Where did the children in the picture get their dark eyes?

Investigate How does a caterpillar grow and change?

Living things change as they grow. Some insects look different from their parents.

Egg

Larva

Adult

Chrysalis

Materials

caterpillars

butterfly habitat

crayons and markers

What to Do

1 Observe your caterpillars every day. **Collect data** every day for 3 weeks.

Monday
The caterpillars are little. They don't move a lot.

Tuesday
They look the same. They move a lot. They are eating.

2 Look for a chrysalis to form. Your teacher will put the chrysalis in the butterfly habitat.

3 Continue to collect data. **Predict** what will happen next.

They're alive! Handle with care.

4 Draw pictures that show how the caterpillars changed.

☐ → ☐ → ☐

Explain Your Results

1. How did the caterpillars change?
2. **Infer** What happens inside a chrysalis?

Go Further

Can you make a model of how a caterpillar grows and changes? Try it.

Measuring Time

These pictures show the life cycle of a butterfly and the life cycle of a frog. They show the amount of time between each step in the life cycles.

A butterfly life cycle

4. butterfly

1. egg

14 days

4 days

12 days

3. pupa

2. caterpillar

eTools Take It to the Net
pearsonsuccessnet.com

1. How many days does it take a butterfly egg to hatch into a caterpillar?

2. How many days does it take for a butterfly egg to become a butterfly? Write a number sentence.

3. It takes 2 weeks for frog eggs to hatch into tadpoles. How many days is this? Write a number sentence.

A frog life cycle

1. egg

2 weeks

16 weeks

3. frog

2. tadpole

Lab zone **Take-Home Activity**

A caterpillar grows to be about 5 centimeters long. What other things might be 5 centimeters long? Measure to find out.

Vocabulary

Which picture goes with each word?

1. seed coat
2. life cycle
3. nymph
4. seedling

What did you learn?

5. How are people alike and different?

6. Compare the life cycles of a dragonfly and a horse. How are they alike and different?

7. What does germinate mean?

8. Infer Why does a baby turtle's special tooth fall out after it hatches from the egg?

Infer

9. People are wearing heavy coats and hats outside. They are wearing gloves and scarves. What can you **infer** about the weather?

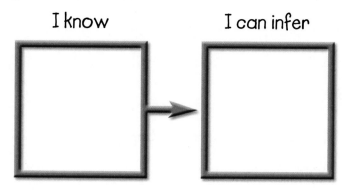

I know   →   I can infer

Test Prep

Fill in the circle next to the correct answer.

10. What kind of animal changes from an egg to a nymph?

Ⓐ mammal

Ⓑ insect

Ⓒ reptile

Ⓓ bird

11. Writing in Science How might living things be like their parents? Make a list.

SAVE the Sea Turtles

Meet Mario J. Mota

Read Together

Dr. Mota

Dr. Mario Mota is a marine biologist. He works at NASA. Dr. Mota studies turtle biology. He uses some of the tools used on the space shuttle to study the turtles.

Dr. Mota was born in Africa. When Dr. Mota was young, he liked to fish. Dr. Mota always loved the ocean. He knew he wanted to work by the ocean.

Sea turtles lay their eggs on or near the same beach where they hatched. They lay more than 100 eggs in each nest!

Lab zone Take-Home Activity

Baby sea turtles hatch from eggs. Work with your family. Make a list of other animals that hatch from eggs.

Find Important Words

There are important words in science questions. These words help you understand the questions.

Megan lives near a big pond where lots of frogs live. One day, Megan sat on the grass by the pond. She liked watching the frogs. Megan saw one frog sitting very still. The frog's tongue zipped out. It caught a tasty insect to eat.

Read the question.

What is one thing that frogs eat?

Ⓐ ponds
Ⓑ sandwiches
Ⓒ grass
Ⓓ insects

First, find important words in the question. The most important words are **frogs** and **eat.** Next, find important words in the text that match the important words in the question. Use the words to answer the question.

Unit A Wrap-Up

Chapter 1

How do plants live in their habitats?
- Plants have adaptations that help them live in different environments.

Chapter 2

How are animals different from each other?
- Animals can be put into two groups. One group of animals has backbones. The other group of animals does not have backbones.

Chapter 3

How do living things help each other?
- Living things help each other in different ways. Animals and plants that need each other for food are part of a food chain.

Chapter 4

How do living things grow in different ways?
- Living things have different life cycles. A life cycle is the way a living thing grows and changes. Plants and animals have life cycles.

Performance Assessment

How Can You Sort Animals?

- Cut out pictures of different animals that live on the land, in water, and in the air.

- Put the animals into groups.

- Tell which animals have backbones and which animals do not have backbones.

Read More About Life Science!

Look for books like these in your library.

heron

cardinal

Experiment Which bird beak can crush seeds?

Look at the heron's beak. Look at the cardinal's beak. How are the beaks alike? How are they different?

Materials

2 clothespins

2 craft sticks

glue

straw pieces

Process Skills

You **control variables** when you change only one thing.

Ask a question.

Which bird uses its beak to crush seeds? **Use models** to learn more.

Make a hypothesis.

Which crushes better, a model of a heron's beak, or a model of a cardinal's beak? Tell what you think.

Plan a fair test.

Be sure to use the same kind of clothespins.

Do your test.

1. Make a model of a heron's beak. Glue 2 craft sticks to a clothespin. Let the glue dry. Use the other clothespin as a model of a cardinal's beak. Use a piece of straw as a model of a seed.

More Lab zone Activities Take It to the Net
pearsonsuccessnet.com

2 Use the heron's beak.
Pick up a seed. Try it again.

3 Use the cardinal's beak.
Pick up a seed. Try it again.

models of seeds

model of a
cardinal's beak

model of a
heron's beak

4 **Observe**. Which beak crushes the seeds?

Collect and record data.

	Did the beak crush the seed? (Circle one for each beak.)
Heron's beak	
Cardinal's beak	

Tell your conclusion.

Which model crushes a straw?
Infer Which bird uses its beak
to crush seeds?

Go Further

Which beak will
pick up seeds
faster? Try it and
find out.

Little Seeds

by Else Holmelund Minarik

Little seeds we sow in spring,
growing while the robins sing,
give us carrots, peas and beans,
tomatoes, pumpkin, squash and greens.

And we pick them,
one and all,
through the summer,
through the fall.

Winter comes, then spring, and then
little seeds we grow again.

Science Fair Projects

Idea 1
Temperature and Seeds

Plan a project. Find out if seeds will grow faster in a warm place or a cold place.

Idea 2
Jumping Insects

Plan a project. Find out if crickets or grasshoppers are better jumpers.

Using Scientific Methods
1. Ask a question.
2. Make a hypothesis.
3. Plan a fair test.
4. Do your test.
5. Collect and record data.
6. Tell your conclusion.
7. Go further.

Metric and Customary Measurement

Science uses the metric system to measure things. Metric measurement is used around the world. Here is how different metric measurements compare to customary measurement.

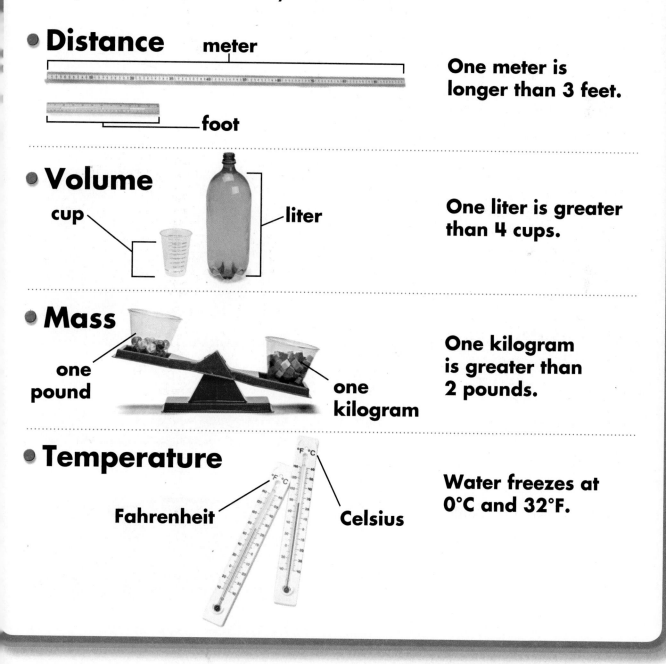

• Distance

meter

foot

One meter is longer than 3 feet.

• Volume

cup

liter

One liter is greater than 4 cups.

• Mass

one pound

one kilogram

One kilogram is greater than 2 pounds.

• Temperature

Fahrenheit

Celsius

Water freezes at 0°C and 32°F.

Glossary

The glossary uses letters and signs to show how words are pronounced. The mark ′ is placed after a syllable with a primary or heavy accent. The mark ′ is placed after a syllable with a secondary or lighter accent.

To hear these words pronounced, listen to the AudioText CD.

adapt (ə dapt′) To change. Animals are **adapted** to live in their environment. (page 16)

amphibian (am fib′ē ən) An animal with bones that lives part of its life on land and part of its life in water. My pet frog is an **amphibian.** (page 41)

attract (ə trakt′) To pull toward. The opposite poles of two magnets will **attract** one another. (page 318)

axis (ak′sis) An imaginary line around which a planet turns. Earth spins on an **axis.** (page 370)

bird (bėrd) An animal with a backbone that has feathers, two legs, and wings. The **bird** flew from place to place searching for food. (page 40)

boulder (bōl′der) A very big rock. The **boulder** is by the water. (page 146)

C

camouflage (kam′ə fläzh) A color or shape that makes a plant or an animal hard to see. Some animals use **camouflage** to hide themselves from danger. (page 42)

condense (kən dens′) To change from a gas to a liquid. Water vapor **condenses** on the outside of my glass of juice. (page 179)

conductor (kən duk′tər) Something that lets heat easily move through it. Metal is a **conductor.** (page 281)

constellation (kon′sta lā′shen) A group of stars that form a picture. I like to search the night sky for **constellations.** (page 376)

consumer (kən sü′mər) A living thing that cannot make its own food. Animals are **consumers.** (page 71)

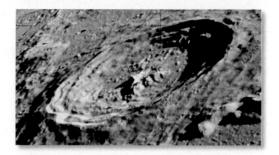

crater (krā′tər) A hole that is shaped like a bowl. There are many **craters** on the surface of the Moon. (page 378)

dinosaur (dī′nə sôr) An extinct animal that lived millions of years ago. **Dinosaurs** are large animals that lived on Earth long ago. (page 212)

E

energy (en′ər jē) The ability to do work or make change. You need **energy** to play soccer. (page 271)

engine (en′jən) A machine that changes energy into force or motion. Cars, trains, and airplanes have an **engine** that helps them run. (page 400)

environment (en vī′rən mənt) Everything that surrounds a living thing. A cactus is a plant that grows in a desert **environment.** (page 16)

erosion (i rō′zhən) Process by which rocks and soil are moved from one place to another. Heavy rains can cause **erosion.** (page 152)

evaporate (i vap′ ə rāt) To change from a liquid to a gas. The puddle of water will **evaporate** and turn into water vapor. (page 179)

extinct (ek stingkt′) An animal or plant no longer living on Earth. Dinosaurs are **extinct.** (page 210)

F

fish (fish) An animal with bones that lives in water and has gills. Many types of **fish** live in an ocean. (page 40)

flower (flou′ər) The part of a plant that makes seeds. Some plants have many **flowers.** (page 9)

food chain (füd chān) Plants use sunlight, air, and water to make food. Animals eat the plants. Other animals eat those animals. This is called a food chain. A coyote and a mountain lion are part of a **food chain.** (page 74)

food web (füd web) A food web is made up of the food chains in a habitat. Corn, voles, and coyotes are part of a **food web.** (page 76)

force (fôrs) A push or pull that makes something move. You use **force** to move the wagon. (page 304)

fossil (fos′əl) A print or remains of a plant or animal that lived long ago. Dinosaur **fossils** are in the museum. (page 207)

friction (frik′shən) A force that slows down or stops moving objects. A bicycle's brakes use **friction** to slow down. (page 312)

fuel (fyü′əl) Anything that is burned to make heat or power. We use wood as **fuel**. (page 279)

gas (gas) Matter that always takes the size and shape of its container. Bubbles are filled with **gas.** (page 246)

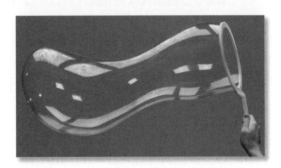

germinate (jėr′mə nāt) To begin to grow into a young plant. The plant seeds will soon **germinate.** (page 114)

gills (gilz) Special body parts that get oxygen from water. Fish have **gills**. (page 46)

gravity (grav′ə tē) A force that pulls things toward the center of Earth. **Gravity** will pull the leaves back to Earth. (page 306)

hibernate (hī′bər nāt) To spend all winter sleeping or resting. Some animals **hibernate**. (page 186)

hurricane (hėr′ə kān) A storm that starts over warm ocean waters that has hard rain and very strong winds. A **hurricane** causes heavy rain and strong winds. (page 192)

insect (in′sekt) An animal without bones that has three body parts and six legs. It's fun to watch **insects.** (page 52)

invent (in vent′) To make something for the first time. Alexander Graham Bell **invented** the telephone. (page 399)

(page 399)

L

leaves (lēvz) Parts of a plant that use sunlight, air, nutrients, and water to make food for the plant. The **leaves** on the plant are long and thin. (page 8)

life cycle (līf sī′kəl) The way a living thing grows and changes. We studied the **life cycle** of a turtle. (page 106)

lightning (līt′ning) A flash of electricity in the sky. We watched **lightning** flash across the sky. (page 188)

liquid (lik′wid) Matter that does not have its own shape, but does have its own mass. **Liquids** take the shape of their containers. (page 244)

loudness (loud′nəs) How loud or soft a sound is. The **loudness** of some sounds can change. (page 336)

mammal (mam′əl) An animal with bones that usually has hair or fur on its body and feeds milk to its young. Chipmunks are **mammals.** (page 40)

manufacture (man′yə fak′chər) To make by hand or machine. Many countries in the world **manufacture** clothing. (page 408)

mass (mas) The amount of matter in an object. I use a balance to measure **mass.** (page 239)

meteorologist (mē/tē ə rol/ə jist) A person who studies weather. The **meteorologist** predicted sunny weather. (page 407)

migrate (mī/grāt) To move from one place to another in a regular pattern. Many types of birds **migrate** in the winter. (page 184)

mineral (min/ər əl) A nonliving solid that comes from Earth. Copper is a **mineral.** (page 147)

mixture (miks/chər) Something made up of two or more kinds of matter that do not change. Fruit salad is a **mixture** of different fruits. (page 250)

motion (mō′shen) Motion is the act of moving. A merry-go-round moves in a circular **motion.** (page 303)

natural resource (nach′ər əl rē′sôrs) A useful thing that comes from nature. Rocks are **natural resources.** (page 143)

nutrients (nü′trē ənt) Materials that living things need to live and grow. People get **nutrients** from the food they eat. (page 7)

nymph (nimf) A young insect that looks like its parent and grows wings as it changes. We found a dragonfly **nymph** in the pond by our school. (page 108)

orbit (ôr′bit) The path around
something. It takes Earth about
one year to orbit the Sun one
time. (page 374)

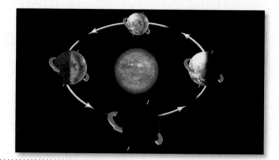

paleontologist (pā′lē on tol′ə jist)
A scientist who studies fossils.
Paleontologists study fossils
to learn about life long ago.
(page 207)

phase (fāz) The shape of the
lighted part of the Moon. The
Moon's **phases** can be seen
best at night. (page 381)

pitch (pich) How high or low a
sound is. The sound from the
bullfrog had a low **pitch.**
(page 338)

pollution (pə lü′ shən) Anything harmful added to land, air, or water. Many people work hard to reduce **pollution.** (page 154)

prairie (prâr′ē) Flat land covered with grasses and having few trees. A **prairie** has a lot of grass and few trees. (page 20)

predator (pred′ə tər) An animal that catches and eats another animal for food. A lion is a **predator.** (page 75)

prey (prā) An animal that is caught and eaten for food. Sea stars are the **prey** of sea otters. (page 75)

producer (prə dü′sər) A living thing that makes its own food. A kelp is a **producer.** (page 71)

property (prop′ər tē) Something about an object that you can observe with your senses. An object's color is one kind of **property.** (page 240)

R

recycle (rē sī′kəl) To change something so that it can be used again. My family **recycles** plastic bottles. (page 156)

reflect (ri flekt′) To bounce off of something. A mirror can **reflect** light. (page 282)

repel (ri pel′) To push away. The north ends of magnets will **repel** one another. (page 318)

reptile (rep′tīl) An animal with bones that has dry, scaly skin. Snakes are **reptiles.** (page 41)

roots (rüts) Parts of a plant that hold the plant in place and that take in water and nutrients from the soil. The **roots** of the old oak tree are deep inside the ground. (page 8)

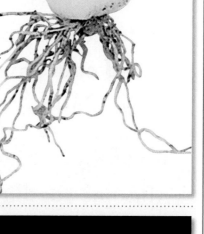

rotation (rō tā′shən) Spinning on an axis. Earth makes one complete **rotation** each day. (page 370)

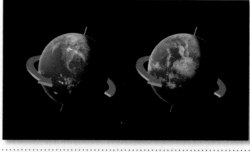

sand (sand) Tiny pieces of rock. People use **sand** to build roads. (page 146)

satellite (sat′l īt) An object that revolves around another object. Meteorologists study pictures taken by **satellites** to predict weather. (page 407)

seed coat (sēd kōt) The hard outer covering of a seed. The **seed coat** protects the seed. (page 114)

seedling (sēd′ling) A young plant. The tree **seedling** grows into a tree. (page 114)

shadow (shad′ō) A shadow is made when something blocks the light. The tree makes a **shadow.** (page 284)

simple machine (sim′pəl mə shēn) A tool with few or no moving parts that makes work easier. Workers often use **simple machines** to help them build things. (page 314)

solar energy (sō′lər en′ərjē) Solar energy is heat and light from the Sun. The house is heated by **solar energy.** (page 272)

solar system (sō'lər sis'tem)
The Sun, the planets and their
moons, and other objects that
orbit the Sun. Earth is in our
solar system. (page 382)

solid (sol'id) Matter that has its
own shape and takes up space.
The case that hold the supplies is
a **solid.** (page 242)

source (sôrs) A place from which
something comes. A lamp is one
source of light. (page 278)

states of matter (stāts uv mat'ər)
The three states of matter are
solids, liquids, and gases. Water
is a liquid **state of matter.**
(page 242)

stem (stem) Part of a plant that
holds it up and that carries water
and nutrients to the leaves. The
stem is long and green. (page 8)

technology (tek nol′ə jē) Using
science to help solve problems.
People use **technology**
every day. (page 399)

tornado (tôr nā′ dō) Very strong
wind that comes down from
clouds in the shape of a funnel. A
tornado touched down near our
town. (page 190)

transportation (tran′spər tā′ shən)
Ways to move people or things
from place to place. Today,
transportation makes travel
easier and faster than ever before.
(page 400)

V

vaccine (vak sēn′) Medicine
that can help prevent a disease.
Mia got a shot of the flu **vaccine.**
(page 402)

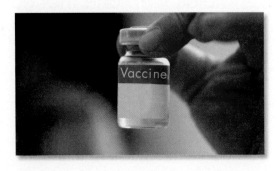

vibrate (vī′brāt) To move back and forth very fast. A flute makes the air **vibrate** to make sounds. (page 335)

 W

water cycle (wȯ′tər sī′kəl) The way water moves from the clouds to Earth and back to the clouds. Water condenses and evaporates during the **water cycle.** (page 178)

weathering (weᴛн′ər ing) The breaking apart and changing of rocks. **Weathering** causes sharp rocks to become smooth. (page 153)

work (wėrk) When force moves an object. It took a lot of **work** to push the sled up the hill. (page 308)

Index

This Index lists the pages on which topics appear in this book. Page numbers after a *p* refer to a photograph. Page numbers after a *c* refer to a chart or graph.

Credits

Text

"Little Seeds" from *The Winds that Come From Far Away and Other Poems* by Else Holmelund Minarik. Copyright ©1964 by Else Holmelund Minarik. Used by permission of HarperCollins Publishers.

"The Spring Wind" from *River Winding: Poems* by Charlotte Zolotow; Copyright ©1970 by Charlotte Zolotow. Reprinted by permission of Scott Treimel, NY.

"This Happy Day" from *The Little Hill* by Harry Behn (Harcourt Brace, 1949).

"Apple Shadows" reprinted from *Black Earth, Gold Sun* by Patricia Hubbell with permission of Marshall Cavendish. Copyright ©2001 by Cavendish Children's Books.

Illustrations

29, 301, 327, 362, 367–368, 370–374, 376, 378, 380, 382, 388 Bob Kayganich; 69 Patrick Gnan; 201–203, 205-208 Big Sesh Studios; 344 Philip Williams; 365 Mary Teichman.

Photographs

Every effort has been made to secure permission and provide appropriate credit for photographic material. The publisher deeply regrets any omission and pledges to correct errors called to its attention in subsequent editions.

Unless otherwise acknowledged, all photographs are the property of Scott Foresman, a division of Pearson Education.

Photo locators denoted as follows: Top (T), Center (C), Bottom (B), Left (L), Right (R), Background (Bkgd).

Cover: (C) ©Chase Swift/Corbis, (B) ©Walter Hodges/Corbis, (Bkgd) ©Ralph A. Clevenger/Corbis, (Bkgd) ©George Grall/NGS Image Collection

Title Page: ©Tom Brakefield/Corbis

Front Matter: ii ©DK Images; iii (TR, BR) ©DK Images; v ©DK Images; vi (CL) ©David Middleton/NHPA Limited, (CL) ©Stephen Dalton/NHPA Limited; vii (CR) Tom Brakefield/Corbis, (B) Geoff Moon; Frank Lane Picture Agency/Corbis; viii (CL) Nigel J. Dennis/NHPA Limited, (B) William Bernard/Corbis; ix Andy Rouse/NHPA Limited; x (CL) ©Stone/Getty Images, (CL) ©Steve Terrill/Corbis, (B) ©DK Images; xi ©Jim Zuckerman/Corbis; xiii ©DK Images; xiv ©Charles Gupton/Corbis; xv ©Kelly-Mooney Photography/Corbis; xvi (CL) ©Lester Lefkowitz/Corbis, (CL) Getty Images; xvii (CR) ©John Gillmoure/Corbis, (Bkgd) ©Handout/Reuters/Corbis; xviii (CL, B) NASA Image Exchange, (CL) Getty Images, (BC) ©NASA/JPL/Handout/Reuters/Corbis; xix ©Reuters/Corbis; xxiv NASA; xxv Getty Images; xxix ©Royalty-Free/Corbis; xxxi ©Ed Bock/Corbis.

Unit A: Divider: (Bkgd) Digital Vision, (CC) Digital Vision; **Chapter 1:** 1 (C) ©David Middleton/NHPA Limited, (BR) ©Stephen Dalton/NHPA Limited, (TR) Brand X Pictures; 2 (BR) ©DK Images, (T) Corbis; 3 (BL) ©DK Images, (BR) Richard Hamilton Smith/Corbis; 5 (Bkgd) Corbis, (CL) ©Stephen Dalton/NHPA Limited, (CL) ©Eric Crichton/Corbis; 6 (C) Corbis, (TR) ©Stephen Dalton/NHPA Limited; 7 (BR) Brand X Pictures, (TR) Hemera Technologies; 8 (TL, BL, BC) ©DK Images; 10 Brand X Pictures; 11 (CL) ©Ted Mead/PhotoLibrary, (TR, BR) ©DK Images, (TL) ©Michael Boys/Corbis, (CR) ©ChromaZone Images/Index Stock Imagery, (BL) ©Scott Camazine/Photo Researchers, Inc.; 12 (TL) Peter Anderson/©DK Images, (CR) ©Cosmo Condina/Getty Images; 13 (CL) Steve Kaufman/Corbis, (CR) Ted Levin/Animals Animals/Earth Scenes; 14 Getty Images; 15 (TR, CR) ©DK Images, (TL) ©Bill Ross/Corbis, (CL) ©Ed Reschke/Peter Arnold, Inc., (BL) ©Ted Mead/PhotoLibrary, (BR) Getty Images; 16 (CR) ©M.P. Kahl/DRK Photo, (TL) ©DK Images; 17 (CL)©Royalty-Free/Corbis, (TR) ©DK Images; 18 (TL) ©Medford Taylor/NGS Image Collection, (BR) ©Eric Crichton/Corbis; 19 (TR, BR) ©DK Images, (C) ©Bob Wickham/PhotoLibrary; 20 (TL) ©Pat O'Hara/Corbis, (BR) Neil Fletcher and Matthew Ward/©DK Images; 21 (C) Getty Images, (BR) ©Pat O'Hara/Corbis, (BR) ©David Muench/Corbis; 22 (BR) ©Ronald Martin, (TL) Getty Images; 23 (C) Randall Hyman Photography, (BR) ©Patti Murray/Animals Animals/Earth Scenes, (TR) ©Steve Kaufman/Corbis; 24 (TL, BR) Brand X Pictures; 25 (TR) Image Quest 3-D/NHPA Limited, (BR) ©OSF/Animals Animals/Earth Scenes, ©David Muench/

Corbis; 26 ©George D. Lepp/Corbis; 28 (CL, BL) Matthew Ward/©DK Images, (T) Hemera Technologies; 29 ©Klein/Hubert/Peter Arnold, Inc.; 30 (BR) ©Pat O'Hara/Corbis, (TR) ©Richard Hamilton Smith/Corbis, (TL, CL, CC, CR) ©DK Images; 31 (TR) ©DK Images, (CL) ©Roy Rainford/Robert Harding Picture Library, Ltd.; 32 (BL) Getty Images, (TL, CL) Hunt Institute for Botanical Documentation/Carnegie Mellon University, Pittsburgh, PA; **Chapter 2:** 33 (C) Tom Brakefield/Corbis, (CR) Brand X Pictures; 34 (BL) ©Don Enger/Animals Animals/Earth Scenes, (TC) ©Alan G. Nelson/Animals Animals/Earth Scenes, (BR) Getty Images; 35 (CR) ©Tom Brakefield/Corbis, (TR) ©Joe McDonald/Corbis, (BR) ©Buddy Mays/Corbis, (BL) ©Jean-Louis Le Moigne/NHPA Limited; 37 (Bkgd) ©Alan G. Nelson/Animals Animals/Earth Scenes, (TR) Brand X Pictures, (CL) ©Breck P. Kent/Animals Animals/Earth Scenes, (BCL) ©Joe McDonald/Animals Animals/Earth Scenes; 38 ©Alan G. Nelson/Animals Animals/Earth Scenes; 39 (BR) ©W. Perry Conway/Corbis, (TL) ©DK Images; 40 (BL) ©Joe McDonald/Corbis, (BC) ©George D.Lepp/Corbis, (BR) Getty Images, (TL) Hemera Technologies; 41 (BL) Getty Images, (BR) ©Tom Brakefield/Corbis; 42 (BL) ©Royalty-Free/Corbis, (TR) ©Joe McDonald/Corbis, (TL) Getty Images, ©D. Robert & Lorri Franz/Corbis; 43 ©Breck P. Kent/Animals Animals/Earth Scenes; 44 (TR) ©Jean-Louis Le Moigne/NHPA Limited, (B) ©Kent Wood/Photo Researchers, Inc., (TL) ©DK Images; 45 ©DK Images; 46 (CR, BL) ©DK Images, (TL) ©Comstock; 47 (TR, CR) ©DK Images; 48 (C) ©Stephen Dalton/NHPA Limited, (BL) ©Daniel Heuclin/NHPA Limited, (TL) Hemera Technologies; 49 ©Zig Leszczynski/Animals Animals/Earth Scenes; 50 (B) ©Carmela Leszczynski/Animals Animals/Earth Scenes, (TL) Hemera Technologies; 51 (CL) Getty Images, (C) ©Kim Taylor/Bruce Coleman Collection; 52 (TL, C) ©DK Images, (BL) ©Geoff Moon/Frank Lane Picture Agency/Corbis; 53 ©OSF/D. Clyne/Animals Animals/Earth Scenes; 54 (TL, C) ©DK Images; 55 (CR) ©Niall Benvie/Corbis, (TR, CR)©DK Images; 56 ©Dale Sanders/Masterfile Corporation; 58 (C, BC, BR) ©DK Images, (BL) ©Royalty-Free/Corbis, (CL) ©Carmela Leszczynski/Animals Animals/Earth Scenes; 59 (BL) ©DK Images, (BR) ©Daniel Heuclin/NHPA Limited; 60 (TR, CL, BR) Getty Images, (TL) ©Tom Brakefield/Corbis, (TCL) ©DK Images, (TCR) ©Joe McDonald/Corbis, (CR) ©Don Enger/Animals Animals/Earth Scenes; 61 (TR) ©DK Images, (CL, CR) Hemera Technologies; 62 (Bkgd) Map Resources, (C) ©Marian Bacon/Animals Animals/Earth Scenes, (B) Getty Images; 63 (TR) ©Andrew Syred/Photo Researchers, Inc., (T)©Royalty-Free/Corbis, (BR) MFSC/NASA, (C) ©Orbital Sciences Corporation/Photo Researchers, Inc.; 64 (BL) ©Niall Benvie/Corbis, (CL)©George Grall/National Geographic/Getty Images, (TR) ©Raymond Gehman/NGS Image Collection; **Chapter 3:** 65 (TC) ©Nigel J. Dennis/NHPA Limited, (TR) Getty Images; 66 (TC) ©Clem Haagner/Gallo Images/Corbis, (B) ©Kennan Ward/Corbis; 67 (BR) ©Randy Morse/Animals Animals/Earth Scenes, (CR) ©Stephen Frink/Corbis, (BR) ©James Watt/Animals Animals/Earth Scenes, (CR) ©Steve Bein/Corbis, (CR) ©Andrew J. Martinez/Photo Researchers, Inc., (TR) ©Sanford/Agliolo/Corbis, (TR) ©Amos Nachoum/Corbis; 69 (Bkgd) ©Clem Haagner/Gallo Images/Corbis, (TR) Getty Images; 70 Clem Haagner/Gallo Images/Corbis; 71 (R) ©Peter Johnson/Corbis, (TR) Hemera Technologies; 72 (TL) Getty Images, (B) ©Clem Haagner/Gallo Images/Corbis; 73 ©Ian Beames/Ecoscene/Corbis; 74 (BL) ©Royalty-Free/Corbis, (BR) ©Joe McDonald/Corbis, (TL) Frank Greenaway/©DK Images; 75 (BR) ©William Bernard/Corbis, ©Gaoil Shumway/Getty Images, (CR) ©Royalty-Free/Corbis; 76 (TR) ©DK Images, (TL, CR) ©Joe McDonald/Corbis, (BR) ©Stephen Krasemann/NHPA Limited, (CL)©Royalty-Free/Corbis; 77 (CL) ©Gaoil Shumway/Getty Images, (TC) ©Jim Zipp/Photo Researchers, Inc.; 78 (CL) ©Randy Morse/Animals Animals/Earth Scenes, (BC) ©Stephen Frink/Corbis, (CR) ©Andrew J. Martinez/Photo Researchers, Inc., (TL) Brand X Pictures; 79 ©Kennan Ward/Corbis; 80 (TC) ©James Watt/Animals Animals/Earth Scenes, (BR) ©Andrew J. Martinez/Photo Researchers, Inc., (CR) ©Stephen Frink/Corbis, (CL) ©Randy Morse/Animals Animals/Earth Scenes, (TL) ©Andrew J. Martinez/Photo Researchers, Inc.; 81 (T) ©Amos Nachoum/Corbis, (CR) ©Sanford/Agliolo/Corbis, (BC) ©Steve Bein/Corbis; 82 (T) ©Sanford/Agliolo/Corbis, (BL) ©Bettmann/Corbis; 83 ©Sanford/Agliolo/Corbis; 84 (B) ©Michael and Patricia Fogden/Corbis, (TL) ©DK Images; 85 ©Fred McConnaughey/Photo Researchers, Inc.; 86 (BL) ©Darrell Gulin/Corbis, (TL) Getty Images, (BR) ©Farrell Grehan/Corbis; 87 ©DK Images; 88 (CL) ©Pete Atkinson/NHPA Limited, (TL) NHPA Limited; 89 (CC) ©Eric and David Hosking/Corbis, (TC) ©Rob C. Nunnington/Gallo Images/Corbis, (BR) ©Richard Murphy; 90 ©Kennan Ward/Corbis; 92 (TR) ©Joe McDonald/Corbis, (BR) ©D. Robert and Lorri Franz/Corbis, (BL) Frank Greenaway/©DK Images, (Bkgd) ©William Manning/Corbis, (BL) Getty Images, (CL) Jane Burton/©DK Images; 94 (BR) ©Clem Haagner/Gallo Images/Corbis, (TC) ©Stephen Krasemann/NHPA Limited, (TR) ©Randy Morse/Animals Animals/Earth Scenes, (CL, CR) ©Royalty-Free/Corbis, (C) ©Joe McDonald/Corbis; 95 (CL) ©George H. H. Huey/Corbis, (CR) ©Norbert Rosing/NGS Image Collection, (TR) ©Andrew J. Martinez/Photo Researchers, Inc.; 96